A Year with the
PSALMS

A Year with the PSALMS

365 Meditations and Prayers

Eugene H. Peterson

WORD BOOKS
PUBLISHER
WACO, TEXAS

242. 2
P

A Year with the Psalms

Printed in the United States of America
ISBN 0-8499-0149-9
Library of Congress catalog card number: 79-63943

Unless otherwise noted, all Scripture quotations are from the Revised Standard Version of the Bible, copyright 1946, 1952, © 1971, 1973 by the Division of Christian Education of the National Council of the Churches of Christ in the U.S.A., and are used by permission.

Most of the devotionals in this book appeared in *Today's Christian* and have been reprinted by permission of the Fuller Evangelistic Association.

For information on sources of previously published and copyrighted material, see pages 195–96.

For Jan
who prays with and for me

Prayer . . . [is] reversed thunder.
George Herbert,
"Prayer" (I)

When the Lamb opened the seventh seal, there was
silence in heaven for about half an hour. Then . . . another angel came and stood at the altar with a golden
censer; and he was given much incense to mingle with the
prayers of all the saints upon the golden altar before the
throne; and the smoke of the incense rose with the prayers
of the saints from the hand of the angel before God. Then
the angel took the censer and filled it with fire from the
altar and threw it on the earth; and there were peals of
thunder, voices, flashes of lightning, and an earthquake.
Revelation 8:1–5

Introduction

When the seventh seal is opened in that fusion of vision and prayer which is the Apocalypse, there is silence in heaven for about half an hour. A climax has been reached. The silence prepares the imagination to receive a conclusion. While conflicts raged between good and evil, prayers went up from hunted and huddled bands of first-century Christians all over the Roman Empire. Massive engines of persecution and scorn pummeled the poor and the weak to the point of despair. They had neither weapons nor votes. They had no money and no prestige. But they prayed. Much of what they prayed was lifted from the psalms.

It was in order to hear those prayers that there was silence in heaven. Out of the silence action developed: an angel came before the altar of God with a censer. He mixed the prayers of the Christians with incense (which cleansed them from impurities) and combined them with fire (God's Spirit) from the altar. Then he put it all in the censer and threw it over heaven's ramparts. The censer, plummeting through the air, landed on earth. On impact there were "peals of thunder, voices, flashes of lightning, and an earthquake" (Rev. 8:5). The prayers which had ascended silently and unnoticed are now returned with immense force—"reversed thunder." Prayer reenters history with incalculable effects. Our earth is shaken daily by it.

The vision convinces the Christian of the potencies and necessities of prayer. But even after being convinced, we don't always feel like

9

praying or, feeling like it, are uncertain how to proceed. Prayer is not something to which we bring native skills. We are, alternately, indolent and clumsy.

The psalms, more than anything else in the church's life, are God's provision for such needs, stimulating and shaping the prayers of Christians. They do not do our praying for us—they cannot be mechanized into a prayer wheel—but they get us praying when we don't feel like it, and they train us in prayers that are honest and right. They are both encouragement to pray and patterns of prayer. They represent the experience of men and women who have prayed in every conceivable circumstance across thirty centuries. "The psalms acquire, for those who know how to enter into them, a surprising depth, a marvelous and inexhaustible actuality. They are bread, miraculously provided by Christ, to feed those who have followed Him into the wilderness" (Thomas Merton, *Bread in the Wilderness*, p. 3).

Out of this conviction I have written *A Year with the Psalms*. I hope the book will be both guide and encouragement to the daily prayer that clarifies and deepens our perception of God's will so that we can pursue it, that exposes the shoddy and cheap so that we can reject it, and that nurtures the true, the beautiful, and the good so that we will live at our best with and before God.

The psalms are access to an environment in which God is the pivotal center of life, and all other persons, events or circumstances are third parties. Existence is illuminated in direct relationship to God himself. Neither bane nor blessing distracts the psalmist from this center. He is not misled by demons of Size, Influence, Importance or Power. He turns his back on the gaudy pantheons of Canaan and Assyria and gives himself to personal intensities that become awe and intimacy before God.

For such reasons, among persons who want to pray, the psalms are God's best gift. "In this as in so much else," wrote Baron von Hugel to his niece, "I find that you are one with the church, that you pray the psalms" (*Letters from Baron Friederich von Hugel to a Niece*, p. 185).

1.
"Blessed Is the Man"

Read Psalm 1

> Blessed is the man
>   who walks not in the counsel of the wicked,
>   nor stands in the way of sinners,
>   nor sits in the seat of scoffers;
>   but his delight is in the law of the LORD. . . .
> *Psalm 1:1–2*

The "tree" man has roots deep in God's ways: he delights in them and meditates on them. The "chaff" man won't be entangled in such earthy permanence: "too limiting," he would probably say.

PRAYER: Thank you, God, for both the warning and the promise. The dismal prospects that surround the way of the wicked are nothing to shout about; the happy results of running in the way of your commandments are. Set my feet firmly in such a path, for Jesus' sake. *Amen.*

2.
"Blessed Are All"

Read Psalm 2

> Serve the LORD with fear,
>   with trembling kiss his feet,
> lest he be angry, and you perish in the way;
>   for his wrath is quickly kindled.
> Blessed are all who take refuge in him.
> *Psalm 2:11–12*

If the first psalm is a laser concentration on the individual, the second psalm is a wide-angle lens on humanity. God deals with us personally; he also has public ways that intersect the lives of nations, rulers, kings and governments.

PRAYER: "O God of earth and altar, bow down and hear our cry; our earthly rulers falter, our people drift and die; the walls of gold entomb us, the swords of scorn divide; take not Thy thunder from us, but take away our pride." *Amen.*

(G. K. Chesterton, "O God of Earth and Altar")

3.
"Deliver Me, O My God!"

Read Psalm 3

> I lie down and sleep;
>   I wake again, for the LORD sustains me. . . .
> Arise, O LORD!
> Deliver me, O my God!
> For thou dost smite all my enemies on the cheek,
>   thou dost break the teeth of the wicked.
> *Psalm 3:5, 7*

We do not acquire security by eliminating enemies. Opposition—and sometimes it is intense—is a continuing reality in this world. We get security ("I lie down and sleep . . . I am not afraid") by putting our trust in God. They are *his* foes and he will do battle: "Deliverance belongs to the Lord."

PRAYER: O God, I feel the rising menace of sin: degeneracy in society, disorder in lives around me, sickness, death. None of the precautions I take seems adequate. Deliver me from my fears and lift up my head! *Amen.*

4.
"Joy in My Heart"

Read Psalm 4

> Thou hast put more joy in my heart
>   than they have when their grain and wine abound.
> In peace I will both lie down and sleep;
>   for thou alone, O LORD, makest me dwell in safety.
> *Psalm 4:7–8*

The scattered experiences of the day—distress, indignation, trust, devotion, threat—are assembled in prayer and laid before God, after which the psalmist simply turns over and goes to sleep, joyfully and peacefully.

PRAYER: God of all beginnings and all endings, I bring all my unfinished business to you—everything that I started and couldn't finish, all that I began but lost interest in, all that I began in hope and quit in despair. Make finished work of all of it, by your grace. *Amen.*

5.
"In the Morning Thou Dost Hear My Voice"

Read Psalm 5

O LORD, in the morning thou dost hear my voice;
in the morning I prepare a sacrifice for thee, and watch.
Psalm 5:3

Morning prayer anticipates the day in hope. It is a preview of possibilities: God's actions, personal acts of devotion, the world's ways, the benefits of belief. As the hours of the day unfold, these will provide the scenario.

PRAYER: "Come, my soul, thou must be waking; now is breaking o'er the earth another day: come to Him who made this splendor; see thou render all thy feeble powers can pay." *Amen.*
(Friedrich R. L. von Canitz, "Come, My Soul," trans. by Henry J. Buckoll)

6.
"Sorely Troubled"

Read Psalm 6

Be gracious to me, O LORD, for I am languishing;
O LORD, heal me, for my bones are troubled.
My soul also is sorely troubled.
But thou, O LORD—how long?
Psalm 6:2–3

It is hard to imagine suffering more intense. What caused it? No answer. To trace its origins would trivialize it. What is examined is the experience with God in prayer that moves from hopeless depression to assured acceptance.

PRAYER: You, O Christ, who were despised and rejected by men, know how I feel when, by fault or failure, I am cast into lonely pits of depression. Draw me up from such despair on the thin yet cable-strong rope of prayer to stand on "this great roundabout—the world" and praise you. *Amen.*

(William Cowper, "The Jackdaw")

7.
"Judge Me, O Lord"

Read Psalm 7:1–11

The LORD judges the peoples;
  judge me, O LORD, according to my righteousness
  and according to the integrity that is in me.
                                        Psalm 7:8

No one minds terribly being punished for a wrong he knows he has done. It is the slights, discriminations and rebukes we don't deserve that rankle. We long for God to be our judge, not to escape judgment but so that our judgment will be fair.

PRAYER: O God, judge me. Weigh the evidence of my heart. Throw out the lies and excuses I use to defend disobedience and rebellion. Affirm my attempts at righteousness. In the name of Jesus who is my Advocate. *Amen.*

8.
"His Mischief Returns"

Read Psalm 7:12–17

Behold, the wicked man conceives evil,
  and is pregnant with mischief,
  and brings forth lies.
. . . .
His mischief returns upon his own head,
  and on his own pate his violence descends.
                                    Psalm 7:14, 16

Evil boomerangs. There are principles of justice inherent in moral behavior. Mischievous plans carefully made to bring misfortune to another eventually entrap their maker. Surprise!

PRAYER: Almighty God, judge of all the earth, keep me from ever supposing that I am the judge of others, deciding their worth or conniving in vengeance. My job is to sing your praises and love my neighbor. Help me to stick to my task, for Jesus' sake. *Amen.*

9.
"Little Less Than God"

Read Psalm 8

What is man that thou art mindful of him,
and the son of man that thou dost care for him?

Yet thou hast made him little less than God,
and dost crown him with glory and honor.
Psalm 8:4–5

In physical size man is a midget; in the sidereal universe he is barely noticeable, a speck of cosmic dust. In spiritual significance he is a giant; set in the purposes of God, the Creator of heaven and earth, he is gloriously kinglike.

PRAYER: Lord, I look at the skies and am humbled—I am such a minute item in your creation. Then I listen to your word and am exalted—I am such an honored son! "How majestic is thy name in all the earth!" *Amen.*

10.
"A Stronghold in Times of Trouble"

Read Psalm 9:1–10

The LORD is a stronghold for the oppressed,
a stronghold in times of trouble.
And those who know thy name put their trust in thee,
for thou, O LORD, hast not forsaken those who seek thee.
Psalm 9:9–10

When nations stumble and civilizations collapse, the man who trusts in God, instead of joining the general lament, praises his Lord. He is confident that God knows what he is doing, just as he is sure of being included in God's plan of salvation.

PRAYER: Most high God, I praise you for taking me within the stronghold of your grace where I daily experience your presence and know you are for me in Jesus Christ, in whose name I pray. *Amen.*

11.
"Up From the Gates of Death"

Read Psalm 9:11–20

Be gracious to me, O Lord!
Behold what I suffer from those who hate me,
O thou who liftest me up from the gates of death. . . .
Psalm 9:13

There are conditions in life that seem only a cruel prelude to death. The afflicted, the needy and the poor huddle at the "gates of death" and read only one message: "Abandon hope all ye who enter here" (Dante, *The Divine Comedy, Inferno,* Canto III). Here is another message: "Sing praises to the Lord . . . who does not forget the cry of the afflicted."

PRAYER: Regardless, O God, of the desperate straits in which men find themselves, you have shown yourself willing and able to come to their rescue. For this I praise you—for your mercy, your compassion, your strength. In Jesus' name. *Amen.*

12.
"Arise, O Lord"

Read Psalm 10:1–13

Arise, O Lord; O God, lift up thy hand;
forget not the afflicted.
Psalm 12:12

Why do wicked men have so much apparent success? Why do they "get away" with so much? Why doesn't God interfere? The questions produce the impatient cry ("Arise, O Lord!") which leads to the deeper trust that God is listening to his afflicted and is arranging his justice for all men.

PRAYER: Father, I pray for all who feel that they have been forgotten by you, who feel rejected and alone. Reveal yourself to them as the one who will "bring good tidings to the afflicted" and "bind up the brokenhearted," even in Jesus Christ. *Amen.*

(Isa. 61:1)

The faithless escape—fleeing avoiding difficulties & challenges.

13.
"Yea, Thou Dost Note Trouble and Vexation"
Read Psalm 10:14–18

> Thou dost see; yea, thou dost note trouble and vexation,
>   that thou mayest take it into thy hands;
> the hapless commits himself to thee;
>   thou hast been the helper of the fatherless.
>   *Psalm 10:14*

Prayer puts us in the presence of God where we realize his ways with us; at the same time it trains us in attentiveness to human needs, developing a compassionate response to every kind of distress. Word-lists from the psalms referring to suffering are as extensive as those which express praise.

PRAYER: While I pray, O Lord, help me to be open to every grace from above and sensitive to every need around me. Train me in ways of loving that will bring justice and healing to others, even as you direct me by your Holy Spirit. *Amen.*

14.
"What Can the Righteous Do?"
Read Psalm 11

> In the LORD I take refuge;
>   how can you say to me,
> "Flee like a bird to the mountains;
> . . . .
> if the foundations are destroyed,
>   what can the righteous do"?
>   *Psalm 11:1,3*

Escape, for the Christian, is faithless. It means that he has succumbed to the "nothing-can-be-done" disease and thinks the only thing left to do is save his own skin (or soul). The psalmist will not tolerate such counsel. "Since God is involved in the world," he says, "I will be also."

PRAYER: O God, I don't want to be like the disciples who, in the hour of trial, forsook Jesus and fled. When I feel like escaping, avoiding the difficulties and challenges in life, give me the strength to stand fast, in the name of Jesus who is my rock and my salvation. *Amen.*

15.
"Every One Utters Lies"

Read Psalm 12

Help, LORD; for there is no longer any that is godly;
    for the faithful have vanished from among the sons of men.
Every one utters lies to his neighbor;
    with flattering lips and a double heart they speak.
Psalm 12:1–2

The contrast is between man's lies and God's promises. Man uses words to get his own way, saying whatever he thinks will help him get it. God speaks in promises that are pure without a trace of fantasy or deceit in them.

PRAYER: I thank you, eternal God, that not one of your words to me is bloated by boasting or distorted by flattery. I take each one as simple reality. I believe what you tell me about my salvation and trust your promises, even as you speak to me in the Word made flesh, Jesus Christ. *Amen.*

16.
"How Long, O Lord?"

Read Psalm 13

How long, O LORD? Wilt thou forget me for ever?
How long wilt thou hide thy face from me?
How long must I bear pain in my soul,
    and have sorrow in my heart all the day?
How long shall my enemy be exalted over me?
Psalm 13:1–2

Is it wrong to question God? Not according to this psalmist. But note what happens. We don't get answers to the "how long?" question; God doesn't open his plan book to the curious eyes of impatient sinners. We get something better: the Lord himself, a "very present help in trouble" (Ps. 40:1).

PRAYER: O God, what good would it do me if I did know the answers to the querulous questions with which I badger you? You know what I really need—not more information, but more love; not your timetable, but your presence. Thank you for giving me yourself in Jesus Christ. *Amen.*

17.
"The Fool"

Read Psalm 14

> The fool says in his heart,
> "There is no God."
> They are corrupt, they do abominable deeds,
> there is none that does good.
>
> *Psalm 14:1*

"How much simpler everything would be if there were no God. His laws, his love, his will permeate everything and make it impossible for me to be myself. How much easier to get my own way if I simply do away with him. Good idea. I'll do it. There is no God!" Excellent reasoning—for a fool.

PRAYER: Father in heaven, I pray for the people I know who avoid you and deny you. Help them to realize that you are no cumbersome burden to be endured but grace to be enjoyed in praise. Use me as a witness to such reality, in the name of Jesus. *Amen.*

18.
"He . . . Shall Never Be Moved"

Read Psalm 15

> He who does these things shall never be moved.
> *Psalm 15:5*

Moral habits are like building stones. One by one they are added together to form a solid structure, a character which is "steadfast, immovable, always abounding in the work of the Lord" (1 Cor. 15:58).

PRAYER: Even as you have shown me the way, O Christ, help me to walk in it. Help me to acquire the habits that will make me dependable in your service as I follow in the steps of my Savior. *Amen.*

19.
"I Have a Goodly Heritage"

Read Psalm 16:1–6

The LORD is my chosen portion and my cup;
thou holdest my lot.
The lines have fallen for me in pleasant places;
yea, I have a goodly heritage.
Psalm 16:5–6

Choosing is connecting. When we choose God we do not narrow
our lives, we enlarge them. We make connection with a vast heritage,
a country where God's presence is constant and pleasures abound.

PRAYER: I had no idea, O Lord, your world was so rich and so
vast. I did not know I was heir to such a fortune. In gladness I ex-
plore and enjoy the world where you create and redeem in a pro-
fusion of joy. *Amen.*

20.
"I Shall Not Be Moved"

Read Psalm 16:7–11

I keep the LORD always before me;
because he is at my right hand, I shall not be moved.
Psalm 16:8

Faith builds on foundations that reach to the bedrock of eternity.
Life in God acquires a steadiness which is unaffected by the tremors
of anxiety. Even death cannot shake its repose.

PRAYER: "O Lord, support us all the day long, until the shadows
lengthen and the evening comes, and the busy world is hushed, and
the fever of life is over, and our work is done. Then in Thy mercy
grant us a safe lodging, and a holy rest, and peace at the last; through
Jesus Christ our Lord." *Amen.*

(Book of Common Worship)

21.
"Hear a Just Cause"

Read Psalm 17:1–7

Hear a just cause, O LORD; attend to my cry!
Give ear to my prayer from lips free of deceit!
Psalm 17:1

We can be sure of receiving audience with God in prayer. He will hear us out. We can lay our entire case before him without fear of being interrupted, or hurried, or cut off.

PRAYER: I need to be listened to, O God: listen to me. I need to be understood: understand me. I need to be justified: justify me, for Jesus' sake, in whose name I pray. *Amen.*

22.
"The Apple of the Eye"

Read Psalm 17:8–15

Keep me as the apple of the eye;
hide me in the shadow of thy wings.
Psalm 17:8

With God, no one is just another number. The population explosion doesn't overwhelm him. Each of us is a prized object of affection to be cared for and cherished. His recognition of us makes it possible for us finally to recognize him.

PRAYER: I'll never understand, gracious God, how I can be singled out from the millions of mankind for your love. But I don't need to understand it: I accept it! In Jesus' name. *Amen.*

23.
"The Lord Is My Rock"

Read Psalm 18:1–6

The LORD is my rock, and my fortress, and my deliverer,
my God, my rock, in whom I take refuge,
my shield, and the horn of my salvation, my stronghold.
Psalm 18:2

Strange. No one has ever seen God, let alone touched him. Still, the most "solid" experience men have is with God. This psalm, in a sequence of stunning images and affirmations, recounts the experience.

PRAYER: "While I draw this fleeting breath, when my eyelids close in death, when I soar to worlds unknown, see Thee on Thy judgment throne, Rock of Ages, cleft for me, let me hide myself in Thee." *Amen.*
(Augustus M. Toplady, "Rock of Ages")

24.
"The Earth Reeled and Rocked"

Read Psalm 18:7–15

Then the earth reeled and rocked;
the foundations also of the mountains trembled
and quaked, because he was angry.
Psalm 18:7

Earthquake, thunder, lightning, volcanic eruptions—sudden, violent dislocations of nature's routine—are images of the God who is tremendously active beneath the surface of casually observed life.

PRAYER: Lord, in my little faith I try to reduce you to a convenient size and harness your attributes to my requirements. I need your thundering word to lay the foundations of my world bare so I can see that you are not a convenience to use but the very rock on which I stand. *Amen.*

22

25.
"Out of Many Waters"

Read Psalm 18:16–24

He reached from on high, he took me,
he drew me out of many waters.
Psalm 18:16

We can't save ourselves by pulling on our bootstraps, even when the bootstraps are made of the finest religious leather. But if we can't lift ourselves to God, God can, and does, reach down and lift us to himself.

PRAYER: By your grace, O God, I will simply relax in your salvation, letting you do whatever you need to do to draw me to yourself. Salvation is *your* work, not mine. Thank you, in Jesus' name. *Amen.*

26.
"I Can Leap Over a Wall"

Read Psalm 18:25–30

Yea, by thee I can crush a troop;
and by my God I can leap over a wall.
Psalm 18:29

Salvation produces exuberance. Instead of the sweaty, grinding, moral self-help many associate with the religious life, the psalmist displays the dancing, leaping exhilarations of grace.

PRAYER: Great God: praises explode in my throat! Energies of love spring loose in my hands and feet! All praise to you. All love to my brothers. In the name of Jesus Christ. *Amen.*

27.
"A Wide Place for My Steps"

Read Psalm 18:31–42

> Thou didst give a wide place for my steps under me,
> and my feet did not slip.
> *Psalm 18:36*

"There's a wideness in God's mercy, like the wideness of the sea; there's a kindness in His justice, which is more than liberty. For the love of God is broader than the measures of man's mind; and the heart of the Eternal is most wonderfully kind" (F. W. Faber, "There's a Wideness in God's Mercy").

PRAYER: You delivered me, God, from the tangled and cramped alleys of sin and put me in the spacious country of mercy and justice. Now I have plenty of room to walk in your ways. Assist me to follow "in his steps" even as I pray in Jesus' name. *Amen.*

28.
"Blessed Be My Rock"

Read Psalm 18:43–50

> The LORD lives; and blessed be my rock,
> and exalted be the God of my salvation.
> *Psalm 18:46*

If God's business is deliverance and salvation, man's business is witness and praise—to *say* what happens under a living God and then to *sing* it.

PRAYER: I sing your praises, Redeemer God. You lift me up, you deliver me, you give new strength, you give me good work to do. Because you live, I live. I praise your great name. *Amen.*

29.
"The Meditation of My Heart"

Read Psalm 19

> Let the words of my mouth and the meditation of my heart
> be acceptable in thy sight,
> O LORD, my rock and my redeemer.
>
> *Psalm 19:14*

Two things impress the psalmist: the skies, magnificent with sun and stars, a daily demonstration of God's creativity; and the scriptures, packed with delightful instruction, an unending and dependable source of God's wisdom.

PRAYER: I look at your creation, O God, and see inexhaustible evidence of your power to order and to make. I read your word and find a sure revelation of your will to save and to love. Both *where* I live and *how* I live are your work. Hallelujah! *Amen.*

30.
"Answer"

Read Psalm 20

> The LORD answer you in the day of trouble!
> The name of the God of Jacob
> protect you!
> . . . .
> Give victory to the king, O LORD;
> answer us when we call.
>
> *Psalm 20:1, 9*

The psalm begins and ends with the word *answer* in a key position: the life of faith is dependent upon God's response. If there are no answers, prayer finally dries up. The fact that there is so much praying (and the psalms are a mass of documentation) is evidence that God does respond. He is the God who answers.

PRAYER: It is not so much answers to my questions that I want, O Lord, but answers to my needs. I don't always understand what I need, only that I need you. Answer me in Jesus Christ. *Amen.*

31.
"Your Heart's Desire"

Read Psalm 20:1–5

> May he grant you your heart's desire,
> and fulfil all your plans!
> *Psalm 20:4*

A closer look at Psalm 20 shows that its first half is a series of intercessions for the king. No one can sustain leadership without support of the people's prayers. More important than their taxes, more significant than their industry, more influential than their intelligence, are their prayers. The best thing we can do for another is pray for him or her.

PRAYER: I pray for those set over me in government and church. Strengthen them in their leadership, support them with your grace, keep them open to your justice and mercy, use them as instruments for your will. In Jesus' name. *Amen.*

32.
"Some Boast of Chariots"

Read Psalm 20:6–9

> Some boast of chariots, and some of horses;
> but we boast of the name of the LORD our God.
> *Psalm 20:7*

Answered prayers are occasions for boasting! When God shows himself to be the God who brings victory, the God who enters history and responds to human need with salvation, the proper response is boasting that matures into praise.

PRAYER: "Forbid it, Lord, that I should boast, save in the death of Christ my God: all the vain things that charm me most, I sacrifice them to His blood." *Amen.*

(Isaac Watts, "When I Survey The Wondrous Cross")

26

33.
"Goodly Blessings"

Read Psalm 21:1–7

> In thy strength the king rejoices, O LORD;
> and in thy help how greatly he exults!
> ....
> For thou dost meet him with goodly blessings;
> thou dost set a crown of fine gold upon his head.
> *Psalm 21:1, 3*

We don't *thank* enough because we don't *think* enough. Concentrated remembrance turns up vast quantities of material that derive from God and then are happily reexpressed in thanksgiving.

PRAYER: Thank you, heavenly Father, for centering and surrounding my life with evidence of your steadfast love. You permeate everything with surprises freely given. Thank you in the gracious name of Jesus Christ. *Amen.*

34.
"All Your Enemies"

Read Psalm 12:8–13

> Your hand will find out all your enemies,
> your right hand will find out those who hate you.
> *Psalm 21:8*

The psalmist has a lively sense of the "enemy." But he doesn't fight the enemy, he turns him over to God. Our job is to recognize that there is an enemy and then, in prayer, to trust that God will deal with him.

PRAYER: Keep me, O God, from the easy nonchalance that fails to prepare for the onslaughts of evil. Keep me also from the consuming indignation that attempts to get rid of the wicked by my own strength. In Jesus' name. *Amen.*

35.
"Why Hast Thou Forsaken Me?"

Read Psalm 22:1–5

My God, my God, why hast thou forsaken me?
Why art thou so far from helping me, from the words of my groaning?
Psalm 22:1

Present despair is set against the experience of hope. The psalmist feels that God is far away, and yet, at the same time, remembers similar cries for help that have been faithfully honored. Prayer is strengthened immeasurably when it acquires a memory.

PRAYER: Lord, my emotions are a poor indication of your faithfulness. The way I feel has little to do with the way you work. The answered prayers of my ancestors, the multitude of the faithful, the "praises of Israel"—these are the assurance I need to fix my prayers again in Jesus Christ. *Amen.*

(Ps. 22:3)

36.
"I Am a Worm, and No Man"

Read Psalm 22:6–11

But I am a worm, and no man;
scorned by men, and despised by the people.
. . . .
Yet thou art he who took me from the womb;
thou didst keep me safe upon my mother's breasts.
Psalm 22:6, 9

The degradation of being treated mockingly by men is contrasted with the reassurance of being treated tenderly by God. The way people deal with us matters enormously; the way God handles us matters even more and will finally make all the difference.

PRAYER: Dear God, let me see my life through the lens of your love, and so be able to discern in exact detail what you think of me and what you do for me in Jesus Christ. *Amen.*

28

37.
"Poured Out Like Water"

Read Psalm 22:12–21

> I am poured out like water,
> and all my bones are out of joint;
> my heart is like wax,
> it is melted within my breast.
> *Psalm 12:14*

Jesus on the cross experienced just such hostility and pain. Each cruel detail was etched into the body of our Lord. Crucifixion, though, produced resurrection. The worst that men could do became the occasion for the unbelievable best that God can do.

PRAYER: On the cross, Lord Jesus, you gathered all the hostility and suffering of the world (all *my* hostility and suffering) and made of it a mighty act of salvation and deliverance. Praise your great name! *Amen.*

38.
"Proclaim His Deliverance"

Read Psalm 22:22–31

> Posterity shall serve him;
> men shall tell of the Lord to the coming generation,
> and proclaim his deliverance to a people yet unborn,
> that he has wrought it.
> *Psalm 22:30–31*

It would have been predictable if all the suffering expressed in this psalm finally trickled out in a bitter whine. Instead there is praise—a praise that roars glad approval of God's deliverance.

PRAYER: "Sing praise to God who reigns above, the God of all creation, the God of power, the God of love, the God of our salvation; with healing balm my soul He fills, and every faithless murmur stills: to God all praise and glory." *Amen.*

(Johann J. Schütz, "Sing Praise to God," trans. by Frances E. Cox)

39.
"The Lord Is My Shepherd"

Read Psalm 23

The LORD is my shepherd, I shall not want.
Psalm 23:1

God is like a good shepherd who looks after us in both good times and bad. He is also like a generous host who invites us to live in his house, enjoying its elegance and security.

PRAYER: O God, I accept you as my Shepherd: help me to trust your provisions and follow your leading. I believe you are my Host: help me to relax in your protection and recognize the signs of your presence, in Jesus Christ. *Amen.*

40.
"The Earth Is the Lord's"

Read Psalm 24:1–2

The earth is the LORD's and the fulness thereof,
the world and those who dwell therein;
Psalm 24:1

God designed and brought into being this earth and all that lives on it to provide a place in which he can share his will and his love. God's creation is the perfect environment for experiencing God's redemption.

PRAYER: God, restore my perspective so that I will see you as Creator and Owner and myself as steward and servant, caring for your property in a faithful and reverent way. I want to hear your words of commendation, "good and faithful servant." *Amen.*

(Matt. 25:21, 23)

41.
"Clean Hands and a Pure Heart"

Read Psalm 24:3–6

Who shall ascend the hill of the LORD?
And who shall stand in his holy place?
He who has clean hands and a pure heart. . . .
Psalm 24:3–4

The joyful confidence imparted to us by a good creation is matched by an immense responsibility to live as loved creatures. Our inner (heart) and outer (hands) life are aspects of a single discipleship that responds to God's trustworthiness.

PRAYER: "Redeemer, come! I open wide my heart to Thee; here, Lord, abide. Let me Thy inner presence feel; Thy grace and love in me reveal." *Amen.*

(Georg Weissel, "Lift Up Your Heads, Ye Mighty Gates,"
trans. by Catherine Winkworth)

42.
"Lift Up Your Heads"

Read Psalm 24:7–10

Lift up your heads, O gates!
and be lifted up, O ancient doors!
that the King of glory may come in.
Who is the King of glory?
The LORD, strong and mighty,
the LORD, mighty in battle!
Psalm 24:7–8

Something like this happens every time Christians gather in worship: we come to "seek the face of . . . God"; God, the "King of glory," comes to greet us and bless us in Jesus Christ. The church at worship, with heads lifted up in expectation, is at the summit of earth's fullness.

PRAYER: Almighty God, when I next assemble with fellow Christians in worship, grant that I may not be so taken up with my own plans and anxieties that I miss the proclamation of your presence at the gates and your entrance into our midst as the King of Glory. *Amen.*

43.

"Make Me to Know Thy Ways, O Lord"

Read Psalm 25:1–5

> Make me to know thy ways, O LORD;
> teach me thy paths.
> Lead me in thy truth, and teach me,
> for thou art the God of my salvation;
> for thee I wait all the day long.
> *Psalm 25:4–5*

Trial and error is a poor strategy for learning how to live. The way of faith is illuminated with precedents and examples ("thy ways, O Lord") that can save us both the embarrassment of being foolish and the pain of making mistakes.

PRAYER: O God, even as Abraham "went out, not knowing where he was to go" and arrived at the land of promise by your guidance, so I would make my way believing in your promises and guided by your commandments, looking to Jesus, the "pioneer and perfecter" of my faith. *Amen.*

(Heb. 11:8, 12:2)

44.

"He Instructs Sinners"

Read Psalm 25:6–10

> Good and upright is the LORD;
> therefore he instructs sinners in the way.
> *Psalm 25:8*

God likes our sins even less than our neighbors do. But he treats them far differently. Whereas men reject and condemn us when we are flawed and recalcitrant, God mercifully and patiently "instructs," "leads" and "teaches" us. Our sins are an occasion not for harsh rejection but for loving reconciliation.

PRAYER: I confess my sins to you, O Lord, confident that you will not reject this sinner but find new ways to share your forgiveness and steadfast love, through the mediation of Jesus Christ, my Lord. *Amen.*

32

45.
"The Friendship of the Lord"

Read Psalm 25:11–22

The friendship of the LORD is for those who fear him,
and he makes known to them his covenant.
Psalm 25:14

God is *for* us, not against us. When we realize this we are able to spend our lives growing in God's friendship instead of desperately and furtively trying to avoid his notice.

PRAYER: God, it's hard to get it through my head that while I am yet a sinner, and even while I continue to disappoint you, you steadfastly befriend me in Jesus. But how grateful I am! Thank you, in the name of your Son. *Amen.*

46.
"The Great Congregation"

Read Psalm 26

But as for me, I walk in my integrity;
redeem me, and be gracious to me.
My foot stands on level ground;
in the great congregation I will bless the LORD.
Psalm 26:11–12

Choosing friends is a moral act. The psalmist finds his close associates in the "great congregation" of those who merely seek to be themselves ("I walk in my integrity") and to be influenced by the acts of God.

PRAYER: I know, Lord, that I neither can nor should avoid being with unbelievers—after all, your Son spent considerable time with them. All the same, I need people who will share the deep desires and rich blessings of worship. Thank you for surrounding me with such people in the church, through Jesus Christ. *Amen.*

33

47.
"My Light and My Salvation"

Read Psalm 27:1–6

> The LORD is my light and my salvation;
> whom shall I fear?
> The LORD is the stronghold of my life;
> of whom shall I be afraid?
>
> *Psalm 27:1*

Fear responds to danger by burying us beneath thick layers of self-defense where we can only cower in shadows. Faith responds to danger by trusting God and lives head high out in the open with "shouts of joy" (v. 6).

PRAYER: I refuse, O God, to live fearfully or cautiously. I name my fears one by one and turn them over to you, and find them simply trivial when set alongside your majesty. With lifted head I will live in your light and salvation, through Jesus Christ. *Amen.*

48.
"Wait for the Lord!"

Read Psalm 27:7–14

> I believe that I shall see the goodness of the LORD
> in the land of the living!
> Wait for the LORD;
> be strong, and let your heart take courage;
> yea, wait for the LORD!
>
> *Psalm 27:13–14*

To wait for the Lord is not to stand around lazily, wondering what will turn up next. It is an intense seeking after God and a devout believing in his goodness. He is worth waiting for!

PRAYER: "Come, Lord, and tarry not; bring the long-looked-for day: O why these years of waiting here, these ages of delay? Come, for Thy saints still wait; daily ascends their sigh: the Spirit and the Bride say, 'Come': dost Thou not hear the cry?" *Amen.*

(Horatius Bonar, "Come, Lord, and Tarry Not")

49.
"I am Helped, and My Heart Exults"

Read Psalm 28

The LORD is my strength and my shield;
in him my heart trusts;
so I am helped, and my heart exults,
and with my song I give thanks to him.
Psalm 28:7

This psalm, like much prayer, has a cardiac rhythm: first constricting in need (vv. 1–5) and then expanding in blessing (vv. 6–9). The heart sucks in God's grace and then pumps praise.

PRAYER: Father in heaven, let your Holy Spirit so live in me that I may happily share your love in praising acts and festive speech, in the name of Jesus Christ my Lord. *Amen.*

50.
"The God of Glory Thunders"

✗ Thunder is the forerunner to much Desired Rain. *Read Psalm 29:1–4*

The voice of the LORD is upon the waters;
the God of glory thunders,
the LORD, upon many waters.
Psalm 29:3

The man of faith hears something to which other men are deaf: the voice of God. The voice is heard in a wide range of sound from the "still small voice" that calms the heart to this thunderous boom that inspires awe and wonder.

PRAYER: I don't hear enough of what you say, Lord. Cure my partial deafness so that I may attend to your deep, authoritative word resounding through the world in stormy majesty. *Amen.*

35

51.
"The Voice of the Lord Shakes the Wilderness"

Read Psalm 29:5–11

The voice of the LORD shakes the wilderness.
the LORD shakes the wilderness of Kadesh.
Psalm 29:8

The psalmist takes the most forceful instances of power and glory that he experiences—thunder, lightning, earthquake, storm—and uses them as metaphors of God's word: in such a way the world of nature becomes a parable of the world of grace.

PRAYER: God, your commanding voice in Jesus stilled storms on Galilee and quieted hurricane fears in disciples' hearts. Now train me in trust so that I may put aside my timidity and embrace your mighty word with robust faith. *Amen.*

52.
"Joy Comes with the Morning"

Read Psalm 30:1–5

Sing praises to the LORD, O you his saints,
and give thanks to his holy name.
For his anger is but for a moment,
and his favor is for a lifetime.
Weeping may tarry for the night,
but joy comes with the morning.
Psalm 30:4–5

"The man who in the darkness took in the dark guest to sit by his fireside finds in the morning that she is transfigured and her name is Gladness," (Alexander Maclaren, *The Psalms*, 1:284). Hard experience offered to God results in the discovery that joy and blessing permeate life.

PRAYER: Dear God, you have set joy and salvation all around me. Neither grief nor destruction can hold me in sorrow or despair. I praise you for this day, created for joy, in Jesus Christ. *Amen.*

53.
"Be Thou My Helper!"

Read Psalm 30:6–10

Hear, O Lord, and be gracious to me!
O Lord, be thou my helper!"
Psalm 30:10

The trouble of verses 8–10 is preferable to the prosperity of verse 6: if calm lulls us into a complacency which forgets God, adversity can drive us to God for the help which becomes salvation.

Prayer: In time of trouble, God, let my cry come to you, not as complaint, but as a mighty call for help. Let every storm drive me to the secure haven of your love in Jesus Christ. *Amen.*

54.
"Mourning into Dancing"

Read Psalm 30:11–12

Thou hast turned for me my mourning into dancing;
thou hast loosed my sackcloth
and girded me with gladness.
Psalm 30:11

Anger becomes favor. Weeping is exchanged for joy. Mourning is turned into dancing. Grim sackcloth is discarded for God's garment of gladness. The silent soul suddenly becomes loquacious with praise. These are just some of the changes we experience when we begin, in prayer, to open ourselves to God.

Prayer: "O for a heart to praise my God! a heart from sin set free; a heart that always feels Thy blood, so freely shed for me. . . . Thy nature, gracious Lord, impart; come quickly from above; write Thy new name upon my heart, Thy new, best name of love." *Amen.*
(Charles Wesley, "O for a Heart to Praise My God")

55.
"Rescue Me Speedily!"

Read Psalm 31:1–5

In thee, O LORD, do I seek refuge;
let me never be put to shame;
in thy righteousness deliver me!
Incline thy ear to me,
rescue me speedily!
Be thou a rock of refuge for me,
a strong fortress to save me!
Psalm 31:1–2

If we have only a vague idea of who God is and what he does, we can only hesitantly and tentatively suggest things he might do for us. The clean-cut metaphors ascribed here to God show that the psalmist has a very clear picture of God's nature and will. As a consequence he urgently and confidently presses his claims.

PRAYER: You, O God, have taken all the guesswork out of knowing you. You have revealed yourself clearly and graciously. I come to you now appreciating how capable you are of dealing with me, body and soul, and how single-minded you are in wanting to rescue me in Jesus Christ. *Amen.*

56.
"A Broad Place"

Read Psalm 31:6–8

I will rejoice and be glad for thy steadfast love,
because thou hast seen my affliction,
thou hast taken heed of my adversities,
and hast not delivered me into the hand of the enemy;
thou hast set my feet in a broad place.
Psalm 31:7–8

We need far more living space than we can acquire on our own. Sins—our own and others—crowd in upon us and cramp us into narrow, rutted paths. Salvation sets us down in wide-open fields where we are free to live liberated in Christ.

PRAYER: Father, lead me through the narrow gate into the broad place, through the door which is Jesus Christ into the way, the truth, and the life. *Amen.*

57.
"Terror on Every Side"

Read Psalm 31:9–13

> Yea, I hear the whispering of many—
> terror on every side!—
> as they scheme together against me,
> as they plot to take my life.
> *Psalm 31:13*

The agonizing loneliness of pain and suffering is alleviated when we place each detail before God who is a sympathetic listener. The prayer process enables us to see suffering as God sees it and to begin to participate in his redemption of it. The prophet Jeremiah, who suffered extensively and prayed passionately, used part of this psalm in his prayers (Jer. 20:7–18).

PRAYER: O God, because of Gethsemane and Calvary I know there is neither humiliation nor pain which is beyond the power of your resurrection; I place every hurt before you in the sure hope of your salvation. *Amen.*

58.
"My Times Are in Thy Hand"

Read Psalm 31:14–18

> But I trust in thee, O LORD,
> I say, "Thou art my God."
> My times are in thy hand;
> deliver me from the hand of my enemies and persecutors!
> *Psalm 31:14–15*

Driven to the end of our own resources (and the resources and patience of others) we find that the world can look and sound very much like an enemy "out to get us." The same experience can drive us to a deeper trust in God whereby we can say, "My times are in thy hand."

PRAYER: "Discouraged in the work of life, disheartened by its load, shamed by its failures or its fears, I sink beside the road; but let me only think of Thee and then new heart springs up in me." *Amen.*

(Samuel Longfellow, "I Look to Thee in Every Need")

59.
"The Covert of Thy Presence"

Read Psalm 31:19–20

> In the covert of thy presence thou hidest them
> from the plots of men;
> thou holdest them safe under thy shelter
> from the strife of tongues.
>
> *Psalm 31:20*

The man of faith does not escape *from* reality but *into* reality. As he runs from the "plots of men" and into the "covert of thy presence" it is as if he were running from a cave full of snarling beasts into a wide, lush pasture where the open air and the wide horizons bring the exclamation, "O how abundant is thy goodness!"

PRAYER: "Beneath the cross of Jesus I fain would take my stand—the shadow of a mighty Rock within a weary land; a home within the wilderness, a rest upon the way, from the burning of the noontide heat, and the burden of the day." *Amen.*

(Elizabeth C. Clephane, "Beneath the Cross of Jesus")

60.
"Beset as in a Besieged City"

Read Psalm 31:21–22

> Blessed be the LORD,
> for he has wondrously shown his steadfast love to me
> when I was beset as in a besieged city.
>
> *Psalm 31:21*

A man in trouble is like a city under siege: the very defense system which had been constructed to keep the enemy out is now used to keep the citizen in. Our own defenses, however useful they are for a time, finally become part of our problem. What man needs is not a better defense *against* evil, but a great deliverer *from* it.

PRAYER: "Open now the crystal fountain, whence the healing stream doth flow; let the fire and cloudy pillar lead me all my journey through; strong Deliverer, strong Deliverer, be Thou still my strength and shield, be Thou still my strength and shield." *Amen.*

(William Williams, "Guide Me, O Thou Great Jehovah,"
trans. by Peter Williams)

61.
"Love the Lord"

Love the LORD, all you his saints!
The LORD preserves the faithful,
but abundantly requites him who acts haughtily.
Psalm 31:23

The Christian discovers that when he cries to God for help, he is, in fact, helped. God is trustworthy. Through the years these discoveries accumulate in the heart and produce the triumphant call: "Love the Lord, all you his saints!"

PRAYER: All right, Lord, I will love! You have loved me and proved your love whenever I have called for help. Teach me in Jesus and equip me by your Spirit to love you and to share your love with neighbors, as I pray in the name of Jesus. *Amen.*

62.
"I Will Confess"

Read Psalm 32:1-5

I acknowledged my sin to thee,
and I did not hide my iniquity;
I said, "I will confess my transgressions to the LORD";
then thou didst forgive the guilt of my sin.
Psalm 32:5

If we hold our sins inside, hoping to hide them, they fester and poison our whole system. The only one who can do anything about sin is God. Confession is the act that brings sin out into the open and lets God take care of it.

PRAYER: As I confess my sins to you, merciful Father, help me to be honest and thorough—not holding back, not denying, not making excuses—and so may I know the glad blessing that comes with forgiveness in Jesus Christ. *Amen.*

63.
"Be Not Like a Horse or Mule"

Read Psalm 32:6-11

I will instruct you and teach you
the way you should go;
I will counsel you with my eye upon you.
Be not like a horse or a mule, without understanding,
which must be curbed with bit and bridle,
else it will not keep with you.

Psalm 32:8-9

When we want our way with a mule we do not appeal to its intelligence or its morals: we impose our will with bit and bridle. But God treats us quite differently: he respects us as intelligent beings who can comprehend wise counsel, and he honors us as moral beings who can freely choose between righteous and wicked acts.

PRAYER: I want to be worthy of the dignity you confer upon me, God. I place my mind and my morals before you. Instruct and guide me in the way I should go. *Amen.*

64.
"Praise Befits the Upright"

Read Psalm 33:1-5

Rejoice in the LORD, O you righteous!
Praise befits the upright.

Psalm 33:1

Praise is talking and singing happily about what God has done. It is the language and music that suit man's nature. It brings out the best in us even as it celebrates the best in God.

PRAYER: Let me, God, add my voice to all who praise you. "Great praises are in the air!" I recollect your word; I observe your works; everything is praiseworthy! All praise to Father, Son, and Holy Spirit! *Amen.*

(Richard Eberhardt, "Great Praises")

65.
"He Spoke, and It Came To Be"

Read Psalm 33:6–9

Let all the earth fear the LORD,
  let all the inhabitants of the world stand in awe of him!
For he spoke, and it came to be;
  he commanded, and it stood forth.

Psalm 33:8–9

Do words really make any difference? Does talk ever cause anything to happen? Skeptical questions, rising out of the human experience of separating words and deeds, are quashed by a biblical witness that traces the very world we live in to the word of God.

PRAYER: Surrounded, O God, by men who make promises that they never keep and by people who make statements that they do not mean, I begin to treat words as "mere words." And then I look around at what happens in creation and in salvation when *you* speak, and I'm ready to listen again, especially to the "Word made flesh" in whose name I pray. *Amen.*

(John 1:14)

66.
"Blessed Is the Nation"

Read Psalm 33:10–12

Blessed is the nation whose God is the LORD,
  the people whom he has chosen as his heritage!
Psalm 33:12

Belonging to a nation is not a secular option for people who don't want to belong to God. Being a citizen is not an alternate form of life for people who don't want to be Christians. Nations, as well as individuals, find their proper rule and government under God.

PRAYER: Almighty God, rule this nation with justice and mercy. Under your rule may all men realize the joy of your presence and experience not only your providence but also your redemption, through Jesus Christ. *Amen.*

67.
"The Eye of the Lord"

Read Psalm 33:13–19

Behold, the eye of the LORD is on those who fear him,
on those who hope in his steadfast love. . . .
Psalm 33:18

Not only did the Lord make everything (vv. 6–9), he takes care of it. He did not create the world and then walk off and leave it; he watches over it wisely and lovingly. We are his creatures; we are also his children for whom he provides faithfully.

PRAYER: Your creative work, Almighty God, fills me with awe: such power and such magnificence! Your providence envelops me with hope: such care and such attention! Thank you for being everything to me in Jesus Christ. *Amen.*

68.
"Our Help and Shield"

Read Psalm 33:20–22

Our soul waits for the LORD;
he is our help and shield.
Psalm 33:20

Everyone needs a good defense system. Since there are several from which to choose, we need to discriminate. Will we elect to be defended by our nation with its vast military armaments? Will we choose to be defended by an arrangement of emotional devices that keep others from getting too close? Or will we decide to relax confidently in God, "our help and shield"?

PRAYER: Defend me, Almighty God, from every power of sin. As I learn to trust in your care, I find both gladness of heart and peace of mind. "Let thy steadfast love, O Lord, be upon us, even as we hope in thee." *Amen.*

(Ps. 33:22)

69.
"Let the Afflicted Hear and Be Glad"

Read Psalm 34:1–3

> My soul makes its boast in the LORD;
> let the afflicted hear and be glad.
> *Psalm 34:2*

All the great words of praise come, not from those who have never known suffering, but from those who have known God's help in it. Praising God is not the naïve optimism of the sheltered but the hearty realism of the delivered.

PRAYER: "The Lord I will at all times bless, my mouth His praises shall express; in Him shall all my boasting be, while all the meek rejoice with me. O magnify the Lord with me, let us to praise His name agree; I sought the Lord, He answered me, and from my fears He set me free." *Amen.*

("The Lord I Will at All Times Bless," *The Psalter*, 1912)

70.
"Look to Him, and Be Radiant"

Read Psalm 34:4–6

> I sought the LORD, and he answered me,
> and delivered me from all my fears.
> Look to him, and be radiant;
> so your faces shall never be ashamed.
> *Psalm 34:4–5*

Men hide their faces from God when they suppose that he will disapprove of them. The psalmist has a different experience—he knows that God is on our side, that our needs are his concern and that he hears our cry. Therefore, he says, "Look to him and be radiant!"

PRAYER: Blessed be your name, O God. You never disappoint me; you hear every cry; you satisfy every need; you banish my fears. In Jesus Christ you are in all and have become all to me. Hallelujah! *Amen.*

45

71.
"The Young Lions Suffer Want"

Read Psalm 34:7–10

> The young lions suffer want and hunger;
> but those who seek the LORD lack no good thing.
> *Psalm 34:10*

Youth and vigor are no defense against disaster. The suffering person must not look enviously at the "young lions" who appear not to have a care in the world. Security and gladness come from God. Wholeness of life is reserved for those who share his life.

PRAYER: Father, make me more attentive to the realities of your presence than to the illusions of the world, more trusting in the "angels of the Lord" and less envious of the "young lions." I wait upon you in my need for the wholeness you promise in Jesus Christ, in whose name I pray. *Amen.*

72.
"I Will Teach You . . ."

Read Psalm 34:11–14

> Come, O sons, listen to me,
> I will teach you the fear of the LORD.
> *Psalm 34:11*

Because God has a certain character and engages in specific actions (revealed now in Jesus Christ), we learn what kind of person we can be and what kind of activities we ought to pursue.

PRAYER: Help me, O God, to make the connection between your life and mine, between what you are and what I am, between what you do for me and what that enables me now to do for others, through Jesus Christ. *Amen.*

46

73.
"Near to the Brokenhearted"

Read Psalm 34:15–18

> The LORD is near to the brokenhearted,
> and saves the crushed in spirit.
> *Psalm 34:18*

Sin, not suffering, kills. "To do evil is to suffer evil and all sin is suicide" (Alexander MacLaren, *The Psalms*, 1:330). The wicked man experiences suffering as utter despair, the complete destruction of all that is important to him; the righteous man experiences in it the nearness of God, who preserves his children through every adversity.

PRAYER: Thank you, dear God, for your words of comfort, your acts of deliverance, your healing presence. When I suffer, be to me savior, healer, companion, even in Jesus Christ. *Amen.*

74.
"Many Are the Afflictions"

Read Psalm 34:19–22

> Many are the afflictions of the righteous;
> but the LORD delivers him out of them all.
> *Psalm 34:19*

"Many are the afflictions" but more are the deliverances. Suffering is no sign that God has abandoned us; adversity is no evidence of condemnation. The love of God and his salvation are proof against every affliction.

PRAYER: "O love that wilt not let me go, I rest my weary soul in Thee; I give Thee back the life I owe, that in Thine ocean depths its flow may richer, fuller be." *Amen.*

(George Matheson, "O Love That Wilt Not Let Me Go")

75.
"Contend, O Lord"

Read Psalm 35:1–10

Contend, O LORD, with those who contend with me;
fight against those who fight against me!
Psalm 35:1

The sensitive Christian has times when he feels that the world is in a vast conspiracy to trip him up—divert him from the pursuit of God and the way of faith. At such times nothing less than God himself is adequate for deliverance.

PRAYER: Dear God, when I feel that the world is against me and others are, either by their indifference or hostility, impediments in my way, grant that I may not sink into the quicksand of self-pity, but rather call out vigorously to you to be my Savior, in Jesus' name. *Amen.*

76.
"Malicious Witnesses"

Read Psalm 35:11–18

Malicious witnesses rise up;
they ask me of things that I know not.
They requite me evil for good;
my soul is forlorn.
Psalm 35:11–12

When the psalmist's friends were sick he sympathized with them, feeling their illness almost as if it were his own. Now, when he is sick, they all stand around and cluck their tongues, asking what evil thing he did to bring this calamity upon himself.

PRAYER: O God, I want to be able to treat the ill and unfortunate the way you treat them, not using their illness as a chance to find fault with them or blame them, but as a time to share your compassion and strength in the name of Jesus, the great physician. *Amen.*

77.
"Praise All the Day Long"

Read Psalm 35:19–28

> Then my tongue shall tell of thy righteousness
> and of thy praise all the day long.
> *Psalm 35:28*

Three times in this psalm the cry for God's help anticipates a time of praise (note the "then" in vv. 9, 18, and 28). The psalmist expects help. And he knows what he will do when he gets it. At no time does he become so immersed in his trouble that he cannot see into the future when he will be celebrating God's salvation.

PRAYER: Never, O God, let me lose sight of where I am going with you. Help me to make the transition from talking about my troubles to using my tongue to tell your praise "all the day long" in Jesus' name. *Amen.*

78.
"The River of Thy Delights"

Read Psalm 36

> How precious is thy steadfast love, O God!
> The children of men take refuge in the shadow of thy wings.
> They feast on the abundance of thy house,
> and thou givest them drink from the river of thy delights.
> *Psalm 36:7–8*

The mischief-maker, darkly plotting evil on his narrow bed (v. 4), is finally confined there, paralyzed in his sins (v. 12). God, the salvation-maker, expands his presence majestically through a light-flooded world, sharing abundant life with all who come to him.

PRAYER: Thank you, Father, for waking me to this day in which your light exposes the stingy cheapness of sin and, at the same time, reveals the wild, open beauties of your love in Jesus. *Amen.*

49

79.
"The Desires of Your Heart"

Read Psalm 37:1–4

> Trust in the LORD, and do good;
>   so you will dwell in the land, and enjoy security.
> Take delight in the LORD,
>   and he will give you the desires of your heart.
>
> *Psalm 37:3–4*

We are caught between wanting to *have* what the world offers through greed and to *be* what God has created us in love. This psalm is argument and evidence for casting our lot on God's side. Its warnings ("fret not" and "be not envious") and counsel ("trust" and "take delight") introduce the theme.

PRAYER: Confirm, Almighty God, the deep desires of my heart and fix my purposes in your will so that I may not be distracted by what others flaunt as either pleasure or prosperity, as I pray in the name of Jesus. *Amen.*

80.
"The Meek"

Read Psalm 37:5–13

> But the meek shall possess the land,
>   and delight themselves in abundant prosperity.
>
> *Psalm 37:11*

The meek man is neither timid nor shy. Meekness is a positive quality, a kind of serenity that is the opposite of the fretting impatience which, whenever it sees a wicked man momentarily prospering, jumps to the conclusion that God isn't doing his job.

PRAYER: Great God of peace, I cast my cares upon you. Item by item I turn my anxieties over to you. I commit my way to you in Jesus Christ. *Amen.*

81.
"The Righteous Is Generous"

Read Psalm 37:14–22

The wicked borrows, and cannot pay back.
but the righteous is generous and gives.
Psalm 37:21

The wicked man curves in upon himself. He gathers and hoards. He acquires treasure but it turns out to be moldy stuff and, in the long run, useless. The righteous man expands outwards. His hand is open. He doesn't grasp things but hands them around, lightly touching them with appreciation and passing them on.

PRAYER: Save me from the sin, Lord, that looks upon your world as loot to be plundered. I want to be one of those who, by appreciation and praise, makes creation available and attractive to others, through Jesus Christ. *Amen.*

82.
"The Steps of a Man"

Read Psalm 37:23–33

The steps of a man are from the LORD,
and he establishes him in whose way he delights.
Psalm 37:23

God doesn't abandon us to stumble along the best we can by trial and error. Much of Scripture, and these verses are an example, can be classified as "travel notes"—notations on life's journey as it is traveled in faith.

PRAYER: God, you have given freely of both counsel and example. Give also a strong spirit of perseverance, that I may not falter as I walk the way you have pioneered for me in Jesus Christ. *Amen.*

83.
"Mark the Blameless Man"

Read Psalm 37:34–40

Mark the blameless man, and behold the upright,
for there is posterity for the man of peace.
Psalm 37:37

This psalmist isn't afraid of the data of experience and the evidence of history. "Look around," he says, "at the righteous and the wicked; the common sense evidence of everyday life will convince you that keeping to the ways of God develops the best kind of life."

PRAYER: Sharpen my powers of observation, Lord, so that I can see what is right before my eyes: the flimsiness of the world's propaganda and the solidity of your promises being fulfilled among the righteous, even through Jesus Christ, my Savior. *Amen.*

84.
"Thy Arrows Have Sunk into Me"

Read Psalm 38:1–14

O LORD, rebuke me not in thy anger,
nor chasten me in thy wrath!
For thy arrows have sunk into me,
and thy hand has come down on me.
Psalm 38:1–2

Sin becomes pain in the body and misery in the soul: sin causes suffering. But it also causes prayer. Implicit in the cry to God, however wailing and self-pitying, is a recognition that God can reverse the effects of sin and bring wholeness.

PRAYER: "Lord Jesus, think on me, and purge away my sin; from earthborn passions set me free, and make me pure within." *Amen.*

(Synesius of Cyrene, "Lord Jesus, Think On Me,"
trans. by Allen William Chatfield)

85.
"I Am Sorry for My Sin"

Read Psalm 38:15–22

> For I am ready to fall,
>   and my pain is ever with me.
> I confess my iniquity,
>   I am sorry for my sin.
> *Psalm 38:17–18*

Sin very frequently sets off an inordinate amount of excuse-making and blaming of others. But not here. In this prayer I learn to accept responsibility for my own sin (see v. 5), make an honest confession and then look to God for deliverance.

PRAYER: O Lord, the next time I look for someone else to blame for the troubles my own sins have caused, recall to me the words of this psalm. Help me bravely to acknowledge my faults, submit myself to your judgments and hope in your grace, through Jesus Christ my Lord and Savior. *Amen.*

86.
"As I Mused, the Fire Burned"

Read Psalm 39:1–6

> I was dumb and silent,
>   I held my peace to no avail;
> my distress grew worse,
>   my heart became hot within me.
> As I mused, the fire burned;
>   then I spoke with my tongue.
> *Psalm 39:2–3*

The man is suffering. His first impulse is to complain, but he muzzles the impulse and turns the same energies into an intense, burning meditation on the fleeting brevity of life and his hope in a constant God.

PRAYER: "My grief is turned to gladness, to Thee my thanks I raise, who hast removed my sorrow and girded me with praise; and now, no longer silent, my heart Thy praise will sing; O Lord, my God, forever my thanks to Thee I bring." *Amen.*

("O Lord by Thee Delivered," *The Psalter*, 1912)

87.
"A Sojourner, Like All My Fathers"

Read Psalm 39:7–13

> Hear my prayer, O LORD,
> and give ear to my cry;
> hold not thy peace at my tears!
> For I am thy passing guest,
> a sojourner, like all my fathers.
>
> *Psalm 39:12*

In the lands of the ancient East a "sojourner" had no citizenship rights. He was wholly dependent on the courtesy and goodwill of the people of the land—a precarious and uncertain existence. But when God is the host and man totally dependent on the divine mercy, there is nothing to fear and everything to hope for.

PRAYER: God of the fathers, I have no claims to press and no rights to demand. I throw myself on your mercy, confident of the courtesies of the city of God: "Thou preparest a table before me." *Amen.*

(Ps. 23:5)

88.
"An Open Ear"

Read Psalm 40:1–8

> Sacrifice and offering thou dost not desire;
> but thou hast given me an open ear.
>
> *Psalm 40:6*

The man of faith is not a robot, computer-programmed to go through religious motions. He is characterized as having an "open ear"—as a sensitive creature who listens and responds to the word of God.

PRAYER: Lord, I want to learn to read your Scriptures in a personal way, so that they are words written not *about* others but *to* me, and the result is not information crammed into my head but behavior animated by faith. *Amen.*

89.
"Great Is the Lord!"

Read Psalm 40:9–17

> But may all who seek thee
> rejoice and be glad in thee;
> may those who love thy salvation
> say continually, "Great is the LORD!"
> *Psalm 40:16*

God is not an exhibit like a piece of great art in a museum, so that we can take occasional strolls through the galleries and "ooh" and "ah" at appropriate intervals. We praise him when we are actual participants in his creative works of deliverance.

PRAYER: As I praise you, great God, help me to be both personal and honest. I do not want to parrot generalities I have heard from others but to witness to your saving help in my life, in Jesus' name. *Amen.*

90.
"Blessed Is He Who Considers the Poor!"

Read Psalm 41:1–3

> Blessed is he who considers the poor!
> The LORD delivers him in the day of trouble.
> *Psalm 41:1*

The poor, treated with aversion by some and contempt by others, are surrounded by compassionate attention in Scripture. God's people are taught that the way we treat the poor measures the quality of our love for God. "As you did it to one of the least of these my brethren, you did it to me" (Matt. 25:40).

PRAYER: "Daily our lives would show weakness made strong, toilsome and gloomy ways brightened with song; some deeds of kindness done, some souls by patience won, dear Lord, to Thee, dear Lord to Thee." *Amen.*

(Edwin P. Parker, "Master, No Offering")

91.
"My Bosom Friend"

Read Psalm 41:4–13

Even my bosom friend in whom I trusted,
who ate of my bread, has lifted his heel against me.
Psalm 41:9

The psalm describes the experience of a man whose best friend (so-called) let him down at just the time he needed him most, but whose God did not. From the experience he draws some conclusions that are important to the rest of us.

PRAYER: My best knowledge of you, O God, is not what I read about you in books or hear of you in lectures. It is what I learn when I throw myself on your mercies and experience your power to raise me up in Jesus Christ. Blessed be your great name! *Amen.*

92.
"My Soul Thirsts for God"

Read Psalm 42:1–5

My soul thirsts for God,
for the living God.
When shall I come and behold
the face of God?
Psalm 42:2

God is to the soul what water is to the body: an absolute need, felt intensely. The longing, at the same time that it witnesses to our need for God, is evidence of the reality of the God who is there to fulfill our being.

PRAYER: "As pants the hart for cooling streams when heated in the chase, so longs my soul, O God, for Thee, and Thy refreshing grace." In Jesus' name. *Amen.*

(Nahum Tate and Nicholas Brady, "As Pants the Hart")

93.
"Deep Calls to Deep"

Read Psalm 42:6–11

Deep calls to deep
at the thunder of thy cataracts;
all thy waves and thy billows
have gone over me.
Psalm 42:7

God is not a surface phenomenon, slight and changeable like moods or weather. He comes to us in the depths, sharing what is most eternal in himself with what is most needful in us.

PRAYER: Eternal God, I thank you for getting underneath the surface clamor and frenzy of my life and creating a reality in me that is impervious to oppression, springing up in hope and praising your great name in Jesus Christ. *Amen.*

94.
"Hope in God"

Read Psalm 43

Why are you cast down, O my soul,
and why are you disquieted within me?
Hope in God; for I shall again praise him,
my help and my God.
Psalm 43:5

There is much in the world that conspires to induce a kind of anemia in the man of faith. Discouraged and anxious spirits are given this prescription: "Hope in God." Hope fortifies faith to healthy praise.

PRAYER: "Hope of the world, thou Christ of great compassion, speak to our fearful hearts by conflict rent. Save us, Thy people, from consuming passion, who by our own false hopes and aims are spent." *Amen.*

(Georgia Harkness, "Hope of the World")

95.
"The Days of Old"

Read Psalm 44:1-8

We have heard with our ears, O God,
    our fathers have told us,
what deeds thou didst perform in their days,
    in the days of old.

Psalm 44:1

This psalmist is dismayed by what is happening to his people (vv. 9–13). But he experiences his present trouble in the perspective of the long-term faithfulness and power of God (vv. 1–8). A good memory is a great asset for the Christian.

PRAYER: By your grace, God, I will meet challenges, disappointments, joys and sorrows with a mind packed with lively memories of your power and love, knowing that what you were yesterday you will be today and forever, even in Jesus Christ. *Amen.*

96.
"Sheep for the Slaughter"

Read Psalm 44:9–26

Thou hast made us like sheep for slaughter,
    and hast scattered us among the nations.
Thou hast sold thy people for a trifle,
    demanding no high price for them.

Psalm 44:11–12

The apostle Paul, writing to the Romans (8:36), remembers this psalm and lifts a text from it (v. 22). A comparison between the psalmist and Paul as they write about suffering is a dramatic example of the difference Christ has made.

PRAYER: Reinforce my conviction, Father, that nothing can separate me from your love, that there are no places where you are absent, no times when you are asleep, that you are in all times and all places for me in Jesus Christ. *Amen.*

97.
"A Goodly Theme"

Read Psalm 45

My heart overflows with a goodly theme;
I address my verses to the king;
my tongue is like the pen of a ready scribe.
Psalm 45:1

This psalm has been read by many Christians as if the first part
(vv. 2–9) were adoration to Jesus Christ in all his splendor, and the
second part (vv. 10–17) counsel to the church, urging her to leave
the things of the world for a new life as the bride of Christ.

PRAYER: My heart, too, "overflows with a goodly theme" when I
meditate on your ways, O God. And to think that I am part of your
glory! That you include me in your plans! Receive my grateful
praise, through Jesus, my Savior. *Amen.*

98.
"Refuge and Strength"

Read Psalm 46

God is our refuge and strength,
a very present help in trouble.
Psalm 46:1

The supposedly "solid" things of the world—whether mountains
or nations—are flimsy. Man needs (and gets) something more sub-
stantial than either nature or civilization can provide—a secure habitation in God.

PRAYER: O God, let my moments of prayer be quiet centers in a
noisy world—times when I am conscious of your eternal ways and
know the strength of your presence with me in Jesus Christ. *Amen.*

99.
"Clap Your Hands!"

Read Psalm 47

Clap your hands, all peoples!
Shout to God with loud songs of joy!
Psalm 47:1

There is a noisy exuberance in this psalm that is appropriate to God's people—a kind of holiday parade atmosphere that goes along with the realization that "God is king of all the earth."

PRAYER: Your rule, God, is something to shout about! In my praise I will seek to express all I feel in joy and freedom, sharing with others the sense of celebration you bring, in the name of Christ my King. *Amen.*

100.
"The City of Our God"

Read Psalm 48

Great is the LORD and greatly to be praised
in the city of our God!
His holy mountain, beautiful in elevation,
is the joy of all the earth,
Mount Zion, in the far north,
the city of the great King.
Psalm 48:1–2

We need to be as familiar with the city of God, the place of God's rule ("Number her towers, consider well her ramparts"), as with the town we live in, so that we can point out familiar landmarks to newcomers and provide clear directions for any who ask about "the way, the truth, and the life."

PRAYER: I pause now, O God, and survey my surroundings, aware that I live in the midst of your presence and action. I want to be well-oriented in your ways, not for a moment forgetful of who and where I am because of your love in Jesus Christ. *Amen.*

101.
"No Man Can Ransom Himself"

Read Psalm 49:1–12

Truly no man can ransom himself,
  or give to God the price of his life,
for the ransom of his life is costly,
  and can never suffice.

Psalm 49:7–8

Inflated ideas of human power and importance are reduced to manageable proportions by this astringent meditation: no amount of money can buy off death.

PRAYER: May I never, God, forget that you are my Lord and I am your creation; that however wonderfully you have made me, you have not made me to live to myself or for myself, but to you and for others, even as Jesus Christ did. *Amen.*

102.
"God Will Ransom My Soul"

Read Psalm 49:13–20

But God will ransom my soul from the power of Sheol,
  for he will receive me.

Psalm 49:15

Man has no power over the eternal questions of life and death, but God does. We recognize the limitations of man, not so we can wallow in despair, but so we can hope in God.

PRAYER: Keep me, Almighty God, from a silly reliance on man or money to accomplish life's tasks. I put my trust in you and look to you for my salvation, through Jesus Christ my Lord. *Amen.*

103.
"God Himself Is Judge!"

Read Psalm 50:1–6

The heavens declare his righteousness,
for God himself is judge!
Psalm 50:6

God gathers everyone before him in a great judgment scene. It is
an awesome sight: "God shines forth." Man does not live to himself—
everything he does is in relation to the God who made him and cares
for him.

PRAYER: You know, Lord, how immature I am, not wanting to
think about the consequences of my actions, not wanting to be responsible in my decisions. Help me to grow up in righteousness, not
avoiding responsibility but accepting it gladly for Christ's sake. *Amen.*

104.
"A Sacrifice of Thanksgiving"

Read Psalm 50:7–15

Offer to God a sacrifice of thanksgiving,
and pay your vows to the Most High.
Psalm 50:14

God gets no pleasure from what men bring to him—"the cattle on
a thousand hills" are his already (v. 7). What he cares about are our
attitudes and behavior, our glad spirits of praise to him and our
generosity to others.

PRAYER: Father, you know how easy it is for me to substitute an
exterior religious performance for an interior spiritual concern. How
hollow and empty it must look to you! Help me to shape my words
and acts today in the way you shaped yours towards me in Jesus, in
whose name I pray. *Amen.*

105.
"You Thought That I Was One Like Yourself"
Read Psalm 50:16–23

These things you have done and I have been silent;
you thought that I was one like yourself.
But now I rebuke you, and lay the charge before you.
Psalm 50:21

Calloused hypocrites treat God's patience as indifference and suppose that they can repeat their sins with impunity. But God's restraint in judgment is his patience. He waits for our repentance so that he can offer his love.

PRAYER: "God the Omnipotent! King, who ordainest thunder Thy clarion, the lightning Thy sword; show forth Thy pity on high where Thou reignest: give to us peace in our time, O Lord." *Amen.*

(Henry F. Chorley, "God The Omnipotent")

106.
"Cleanse Me From My Sin!"
Read Psalm 51:1–2

Wash me thoroughly from my iniquity,
and cleanse me from my sin!
Psalm 51:2

Psalms 50 and 51 are a study in contrasts. Psalm 50 chases out every brittle formalism and stuffy hypocrisy: Psalm 51 invites the tenderest movements of penitence and trust. The first is a protest against religion gone bad; the second is a witness to authentic piety.

PRAYER: "Just as I am, without one plea but that Thy blood was shed for me, and that Thou biddest me come to Thee, O Lamb of God, I come. Just as I am, and waiting not to rid my soul of one dark blot, to Thee, whose blood can cleanse each spot, O Lamb of God, I come!" *Amen.*

(Charlotte Elliott, "Just as I Am")

107.
"I Know My Transgressions"

Read Psalm 51:3–9

For I know my transgressions,
and my sin is ever before me.
. . . .
Hide thy face from my sins,
and blot out all my iniquities.
Psalm 51:3, 9

Has sin ever been felt so painfully or expressed so poignantly? Recognition of sin forces an awareness of God and develops an unhesitating trust in God's mercy.

PRAYER: Merciful God, how dependent I am upon your mercy! Everything I am and all I do falls short of your glory. Still, you do not condemn me. Gratefully I live in your grace and experience your forgiveness in Jesus. *Amen.*

108.
"Create in Me a Clean Heart"

Read Psalm 51:10–19

Create in me a clean heart, O God,
and put a new and right spirit within me.
Psalm 51:10

If sin brings us to our knees where God can forgive us, mercy puts us on our feet again so that we can praise God and witness to his ways. Guilt brings us low, but forgiveness lifts us high.

PRAYER: I want more, Lord, than just to be relieved of the burden of my sins; I want a new life—a life that participates creatively in your work in the world, a life that shares healing, reconciling, and praising, for Jesus' sake. *Amen.*

109.
"A Broken and Contrite Heart"

Read Psalm 51:15–19

> The sacrifice acceptable to God is a broken spirit;
> a broken and contrite heart, O God, thou wilt not despise.
> *Psalm 51:17*

Tears of penitence and gladness can flow from the same ducts. Contrition before God is not a fearful cowering of the kind we observe in an abused animal, but an honest openness that is confident of mercy. Penitence and praise are integrated in a single act of devotion.

PRAYER: "Broken, humbled to the dust by Thy wrath and judgment just, let my contrite heart rejoice and in gladness hear Thy voice; from my sins O hide Thy face, blot them out in boundless grace." *Amen.*

("God, Be Merciful to Me," The Psalter, 1912)

110.
"You Love Evil"

Read Psalm 52

> Why do you boast, O mighty man ... ?
> ....
> You love evil more than good,
> and lying more than speaking the truth.
> *Psalm 52:1, 3*

The boastful "mighty man" is warned: there is much more to the world than what he is accustomed to dealing with—there is God. And if he will not love God, he will not continue to live. It is as simple as that.

PRAYER: Father, you have given me words of life; give me also the wisdom and tact to speak a word of warning to friends who are boastfully living as if you did not exist. Use my witness to recall them to your salvation in Jesus Christ. *Amen.*

111.
"There Is None That Does Good"

Read Psalm 53

> They have all fallen away;
>   they are all alike depraved;
> there is none that does good,
>   no, not one.
>   *Psalm 53:3*

The cruelty men do to each other is traced to its origins—hearts which deny God. There is an absence of goodness *among* men because there is an absence of God *within* men.

PRAYER: Dear God, I am neither good enough nor smart enough to love my neighbor; but you can do it through me. Use my body to bring deliverance and rejoicing to someone who has suffered injustice. In Jesus' name. *Amen.*

112.
"Save Me"

Read Psalm 54

> Save me, O God, by thy name,
>   and vindicate me by thy might.
> Hear my prayer, O God;
>   give ear to the words of my mouth.
>   *Psalm 54:1–2*

"Save me" is the most elemental prayer. It is at the heart of biblical religion. It joins man's need with God's action in Jesus, whose name means, literally, "The Lord saves."

PRAYER: Lord, I want this prayer at the center of my life. Everything flows from this one petition as I look to you to deliver me from both my own sins and the sins of others. Make a whole person of me in Jesus Christ. *Amen.*

113.
"I Would Fly Away"

Read Psalm 55:1-11

And I say, "O that I had wings like a dove!
I would fly away and be at rest;
yea, I would wander afar,
I would lodge in the wilderness.
Psalm 55:6-7

Maybe this is the reason God did not give us wings—we would use them, not to obey his commands more quickly, but to escape from unpleasant circumstances.

PRAYER: You know, God, how often I want to get away from it all so I won't have to face a world that spurns your love and rejects your life. But you also know how to give me courage: I wait for your help in Jesus Christ. *Amen.*

114.
"Cast Your Burden on the Lord"

Read Psalm 55:12-23

Cast your burden on the LORD,
and he will sustain you;
he will never permit
the righteous to be moved.
Psalm 55:22

Even his best friend had betrayed him! But having no means to escape, he learned to find victory within his troubles. He learned the release from oppression that comes from utter trust in God, a dependence Christians have learned to associate with Jesus.

PRAYER: Dear God, when I feel betrayed and oppressed, instead of wildly casting about for a way out, lead me into your presence where I can cast my burdens on you and find the peace and renewal I need; through Jesus Christ my Lord. *Amen.*

115.
"My Tears in Thy Bottle!"

Read Psalm 56

> Thou hast kept count of my tossings;
> put thou my tears in thy bottle!
> Are they not in thy book?
>
> *Psalm 56:8*

God is not indifferent to our suffering. He is not so taken up with the vast government of creation that he has no time for our tears. Jesus made the same point when he said "Why, even the hairs of your head are all numbered" (Luke 12:7).

PRAYER: "Thy calmness bends serene above, my restlessness to still; around me flows Thy quickening life, to nerve my faltering will: Thy presence fills my solitude; Thy providence turns all to good." *Amen.*

(Samuel Longfellow, "I Look to Thee in Every Need")

116.
"Storms of Destruction"

Read Psalm 57

> Be merciful to me, O God, be merciful to me,
> for in thee my soul takes refuge;
> in the shadow of thy wings I will take refuge,
> till the storms of destruction pass by.
>
> *Psalm 57:1*

Prayer thrives on contrasts. Destructive storms and devouring lions spar with God's steadfast love and faithfulness. There is no contest. The harsh noises of destruction ("storms and lions") give way to the sung sounds of praise.

PRAYER: O God, wake me out of the nightmare fantasies of sin and temptation that threaten my peace with you, that I may live in the daylight of your purpose and be alert and attentive to your love for me in Jesus Christ, in whose name I pray. *Amen.*

117.
"Your Hands Deal Out Violence"

Read Psalm 58

Do you indeed decree what is right, you gods?
Do you judge the sons of men uprightly?
Nay, in your hearts you devise wrongs;
    your hands deal out violence on earth.
Psalm 58:1–2

"You gods" in verse 1 refers to unjust leaders. The psalmist brings a suit against them for their reeking injustice. The understandable indignation is finally fused by faith into hope in God's righteous judgment.

PRAYER: "Judge eternal, throned in splendor, Lord of Lords and King of Kings, with Thy living fire of judgment purge our land of bitter things; solace all its wide dominion with the healing of Thy wings." *Amen.*

(Henry Scott Holland, "Judge Eternal")

118.
"Deliver Me from My Enemies"

Read Psalm 59:1–10

Deliver me from my enemies, O my God,
    protect me from those who rise up against me.
Psalm 59:1

"Enemy" assumes various forms: the intense opposition of wicked men (as in this psalm), the mild seductions of friends, the defiant pride of the rebellious heart. But whether they are inside or out, ferocious or urbane, the man of faith looks to God for deliverance from them.

PRAYER: Because I am not hunted down and thrown into prison for my faith, I develop a false sense of security. Save me, God, from such complacency. I know that the enemy has not gone away even if he is not conspicuous. "Lead me not into temptation: deliver me from evil." *Amen.*

119.
"O My Strength"

Read Psalm 59:8–17

> But thou, O LORD, dost laugh at them;
> thou dost hold all the nations in derision.
> O my Strength, I will sing praises to thee;
> for thou, O God, art my fortress.
> *Psalm 59:8–9*

A good laugh restores perspective and sanity. This psalm begins with "enemies" everywhere; it ends with relaxed praise. What makes the difference? A good laugh! Divine laughter exposes the silly pretensions of wicked oppressors.

PRAYER: Rescue me, God, from obsessive worries about what might go wrong because of evil men. Develop a hearty cheerfulness in me that is confident of your strength. If you can laugh at the wicked, I can too. *Amen.*

120.
"Thou Hast Been Angry"

Read Psalm 60

> Oh God, thou hast rejected us, broken our defenses;
> thou hast been angry; oh, restore us.
> *Psalm 60:1*

We usually associate the word *anger* with a negative emotion, either petulant or vicious. But there is another kind—a positive energy in God that deals with disobedience and rebellion in a way that brings us blessing.

PRAYER: Merciful God, you express anger against my sin without spite and without vindictiveness: help me to respond to it with brave repentance, in Jesus' name. *Amen.*

121.
"The Rock That Is Higher Than I"

Read Psalm 61

> Lead thou me
> to the rock that is higher than I;
> for thou art my refuge,
> a strong tower against the enemy.
> *Psalm 61:2–3*

Did David pray this as a fugitive from King Saul's madness while at the same time praying for the king's wholeness? Prayer that asks for personal help ("lead thou me to the rock") very naturally leads into prayer that intercedes for others ("prolong the life of the king"). Prayer is not an exclusive concentration on either self or neighbor but a correlation of mutual needs. We get what we need and, at the same time, become a ministry to others' needs.

PRAYER: I don't want to become so preoccupied with my own needs that I forget that others need your help too, dear God. And I don't want to get so concerned about others that I fail to keep my own heart in order before you. Keep me in balance, for Jesus' sake. *Amen.*

122.
"My Soul Waits in Silence"

Read Psalm 62:1–7

> For God alone my soul waits in silence;
> from him comes my salvation.
> He only is my rock and my salvation,
> my fortress; I shall not be greatly moved.
> *Psalm 62:1–2*

Silence sinks a shaft to bedrock. It is the soul's means for descending through the gravel of rebellion and doubt to the solid, quiet reality of God's word.

PRAYER: "Be still, my soul: thy God doth undertake to guide the future as He has the past. Thy hope, thy confidence, let nothing shake; all now mysterious shall be bright at last. Be still, my soul: the waves and winds still know His voice who ruled them while He dwelt below." *Amen.*

(Katherina von Schlegel, "Be Still, My Soul," trans. by Jane L. Borthwick)

123.
"Pour Out Your Heart"

Read Psalm 62:8–12

Trust in him at all times, O people;
pour out your heart before him;
God is a refuge for us.
Psalm 62:8

The soul careens from side to side seeking a way to completion. On one side is the anarchic freedom of the lawless ("men of low estate"): on the other, the secure wealth of the rich ("men of high estate"). But the alternatives are ditches, not highways. The Lord himself is the way to wholeness.

PRAYER: First, God, I imagine that I want to live completely free, a rebel against all restraint—a lawless person. Then I imagine that I want to live completely secure, without any needs—a rich person. You expose both as vain fantasies: I will pour my heart out to you and find both liberty and security, through Jesus Christ. *Amen.*

124.
"My Soul Is Feasted"

Read Psalm 63

My soul is feasted as with marrow and fat,
and my mouth praises thee with joyful lips,
when I think of thee upon my bed,
and meditate on thee in the watches of the night.
Psalm 63:5–6

The most authentic and intense desires can be completed only in relation to God. The same God who created appetites in us has also created the means to their satisfaction.

PRAYER: "I find, I walk, I love, but O the whole of love is but my answer, Lord, to Thee! For Thou wert long beforehand with my soul; always Thou lovedst me." *Amen.*

(Anonymous, "I Sought the Lord")

125.
"My Complaint"

Read Psalm 64

Hear my voice, O God, in my complaint;
preserve my life from dread of the enemy. . . .
Psalm 64:1

We do not have to "dress up," either inwardly or outwardly, when we come to God in prayer. We do not have to hide our anger, suppress our distress, or mask our irritability. It is all right to complain to God.

PRAYER: I am so used to hiding the feelings and thoughts that others might find unacceptable, O God, that I even try to do it with you. Keep me honest in my prayers. You know how to deal with such as me: I do not fear your rejection, and I hope in your salvation, even in Jesus Christ. *Amen.*

126.
"The Hope of All the Ends of the Earth"

Read Psalm 65:1–8

By dread deeds thou dost answer us with deliverance,
O God of our salvation,
who art the hope of all the ends of the earth,
and of the farthest seas. . . .
Psalm 65:5

The experience of salvation leads to a widened conception of God's power and strength: instead of (as some suppose) narrowing a person to a neurotic concern for his own soul, it expands his relation with all that God does everywhere "to the ends of the earth and of the farthest seas."

PRAYER: Almighty God, I want to be in on everything you are doing. I don't want to be tied to my own worries, or confined to my private joys—I want to participate in praise and adoration in all you do, throughout the whole earth, among every people. In Jesus' name. *Amen.*

127.
"Thou Crownest the Year"

Read Psalm 65:9–13

> Thou crownest the year with thy bounty;
>   the tracks of thy chariot drip with fatness.
>   *Psalm 65:11*

The person reconciled to God has eyes to see the hand of God in the soil and the seasons. We learn very little about God from nature, but we see many signs of his bounty there. What we see cues us to join in praise of the God who provides such splendid fertility and stunning beauty.

PRAYER: Father, thank you for this glorious world to live in. You have spared nothing to create a magnificent setting in which I can experience your love and enjoy your salvation. All praise to you in Jesus Christ! *Amen.*

128.
"We Went Through Fire"

Read Psalm 66:1–12

> Thou didst let men ride over our heads;
>   we went through fire and through water;
>   yet thou hast brought us forth to a spacious place.
>   *Psalm 66:12*

Every testing is designed to deepen and develop the life of faith. This psalmist's witness is impressive: he went through the worst that men could do to him; he experienced the best that God willed for him. When he sings he does not catalogue his scars, he pulsates praise.

PRAYER: Almighty God, you rescued from the waters and delivered from fire. Too often, though, I fail to make the connection between what you have done in the glorious past and what you wish to do in me right now. Help me to make the connection through the hours of this day and to sing my joy through Jesus Christ. *Amen.*

74

129.
"If I Had Cherished Iniquity"

Read Psalm 66:13–20

If I had cherished iniquity in my heart,
    the Lord would not have listened.
But truly God has listened;
    he has given heed to the voice of my prayer.
Psalm 66:18–19

The ecstasy of deliverance cuts a channel in which promises may be kept and repentance practiced. The intensities of joy are nurtured, not by seeking new pleasures, but by practicing an old obedience.

PRAYER: Father, I want to learn to use the strength you give me during the extremities of my need in the duties of my ordinary days. Help me to be as open to you when I don't feel I need you as when I do. In the name of Jesus "in whom there is no variation or shadow due to change." *Amen.*

(James 1:17)

130.
"God Has Blessed Us"

Read Psalm 67

The earth has yielded its increase;
    God, our God, has blessed us.
God has blessed us;
    let all the ends of the earth fear him!
Psalm 67:6–7

Blessings are not bribes that God uses to get us to serve him; they are experiences that men have when God saves them. The person immersed in God's salvation finds life overflowing with the blessings of God's creation.

PRAYER: "Lord, bless and pity us, shine on us with Thy face, that all the earth Thy way may know and men may see Thy grace. Thy praise, O gracious God, let all the nations sing; let all men worship Thee with joy and songs of gladness bring." *Amen.*

("Lord, Bless and Pity Us," *The Psalter*, 1912)

131.
"Let God Arise"

Read Psalm 68:1–4

Let God arise, let his enemies be scattered;
let those who hate him flee before him!
Psalm 68:1

This rich (and sometimes enigmatic) psalm is a counter against all anxious religion—the timid and worried view that God is desperately on the defensive. In the spiritual conflict that permeates our experience it is God who is the aggressor. The wicked do well to scurry for cover; the righteous can only be "jubilant with joy" (v. 3).

PRAYER: God of strength, overthrow every tendency to anxiety in my heart, every timid fear, every faithless doubt: I know you are victorious over every sin and all evil. Reign victoriously in me, with the power of the risen Christ. *Amen.*

132.
"Father of the Fatherless"

Read Psalm 68:5–6

Father of the fatherless and protector of widows
is God in his holy habitation.
Psalm 68:5

Wicked men demonstrate their power by oppressing the unfortunate and weak; our righteous God shows his power by dealing with the victim, the outcast and the defenseless in compassion and love.

PRAYER: O God, search out the weak places in my life, the parts of me that are vulnerable and immature. Establish your rule there so that I may grow into wholeness, receiving your strength and expressing it in the love that you revealed in Jesus Christ. *Amen.*

133.
"Rain in Abundance"

Read Psalm 68:7–10

> Rain in abundance, O God, thou didst shed abroad;
> thou didst restore thy heritage as it languished;
> thy flock found a dwelling in it;
> in thy goodness, O God, thou didst provide for the needy.
> *Psalm 68:9–10*

God is not a stingy taskmaster; he is a generous savior. His way of salvation travels perilous paths and confronts fearsome hardship, but it leads to pastures where joy and praise are abundant.

PRAYER: Your mighty acts, O God, have forged a path of discipleship for me. Because you go before me powerfully and compassionately, I follow in joy and in trust, through Jesus Christ. *Amen.*

134.
"They Flee!"

Read Psalm 68:11–14

> The Lord gives the command;
> great is the host of those who bore the tidings:
> "The kings of the armies, they flee, they flee!"
> *Psalm 68:11–12*

The strongholds of evil have been ransacked by the word of God. God's people now have the great privilege of announcing his victory and the great pleasure of enjoying its fruits. We *know* something that we are eager to tell, and we *have* something that we are glad to share.

PRAYER: Great God, your victorious work reverses everything I have ever thought about the world: all the evil I was afraid of is now a reminder of your power; all the things I was greedy for are now spoil to be shared. Thank you, in Jesus' name. *Amen.*

135.
"Who Daily Bears Us Up"

Read Psalm 68:15–20

Blessed be the Lord,
who daily bears us up;
God is our salvation.
Psalm 68:19

God's victories are not mere historical exhibits of his power or doctrinal claims of his rightness; they are what is experienced in history by his people. The God who is raised up raises us up with him.

PRAYER: Dear God, when my shoulders droop and my steps drag, speak your encouraging word. It is not, I know, your will that I carry burdens of anxiety: lift them from my shoulders so that I may lift my eyes to you in glad faith. In Jesus' name. *Amen.*

136.
"I Will Bring Them Back"

Read Psalm 68:21–23

The Lord said,
"I will bring them back from Bashan,
I will bring them back from the depths of the sea."
Psalm 68:22

God delivered Israel from the Egyptians at the Red Sea and gave victory over warlike giants (Og, king of Bashan). God is expert in rescuing his people from formidable dangers. His reputation is documented by memories of salvation, each of them, in Calvin's phrase, a "species of resurrection."

PRAYER: Father, stock my mind with the remembrances of your victories, your resurrection ways among your people, that when I encounter danger or difficulty I may confidently trust your power to save me in Jesus Christ. *Amen.*

137.
"The Processions of My God"

Read Psalm 68:24–27

> Thy solemn processions are seen, O God,
> the processions of my God, my King, into the sanctuary. . . .
> *Psalm 68:24*

Israel continues to teach the church how to worship with exuberance and jubilation. Public worship—the people of God gathering to sing God's praise and acknowledge his lordship—is, every time it occurs, a victory celebration.

PRAYER: Great God, whose name is praised by faithful men and women in every land, take my songs of gratitude and words of witness and fuse them into what all your people celebrate. In the strong name of Jesus Christ. *Amen.*

138.
"Summon Thy Might"

Read Psalm 68:28–31

> Summon thy might, O God;
> show thy strength, O God, thou who hast wrought for us.
> *Psalm 68:28*

The experience of God's resurrection develops an appetite for more of the same. The more God does for us the more we want him to do. Each victory leads to another—we go "from strength to strength" (Ps. 84:7).

PRAYER: That which you have done in me, O God, do in others. Use me as a connection by which others can be brought into relation with your love, your healing, and your salvation. For Jesus' sake. *Amen.*

139.
"Sing to God"

Read Psalm 68:32-35

Sing to God, O kingdoms of the earth;
sing praises to the Lord,
to him who rides in the heavens, the ancient heavens;
lo, he sends forth his voice, his mighty voice.
Psalm 68:32-33

"This superb hymn is unsurpassed, if not unequalled, in grandeur, lyric fire, and sustained rush of triumphant praise. It celebrates a victory; but it is the victory of the God who enters as a conqueror into His sanctuary" (Alexander Maclaren, *The Psalms,* 1:271).

PRAYER: "Let all the world in every corner sing, 'My God and King!' The heavens are not too high, His praise may thither fly; the earth is not too low, His praises there may grow. Let all the world in every corner sing, 'My God and King!' " *Amen.*

(George Herbert, "Let All the World in Every Corner Sing")

140.
"I Sink in Deep Mire"

Read Psalm 69:1-3

Save me, O God!
For the waters have come up to my neck.
I sink in deep mire,
where there is no foothold.
Psalm 69:1-2

Focused prayer is accurate and clear about two things: that man's need is desperate, and that the remedy lies in God. Man's need for help and God's will to save are joined.

PRAYER: Keep me always conscious, Father, of my need and your salvation, of the perils of sin and the mercies of deliverance, of my empty hands and your bountiful grace, through Jesus Christ. *Amen.*

80

141.
"I Have Borne Reproach"

Read Psalm 69:4–8

Let not those who hope in thee be put to shame through me,
O Lord God of hosts;
let not those who seek thee be brought to dishonor through me,
O God of Israel.
For it is for thy sake that I have borne reproach,
that shame has covered my face.

Psalm 69:6–7

Men despise and reject what they do not understand, and they frequently misunderstand righteousness; this means that the righteous man often experiences contempt. Closeness to God sometimes means alienation from men.

PRAYER: Father, you know my inner heart, my secret motives, my basic desires. My sins and my virtues are both under your mercy, so that I have nothing to fear from men and everything to hope from you, even in Jesus Christ. *Amen.*

142.
"Zeal for Thy House"

Read Psalm 69:9–15

For zeal for thy house has consumed me,
and the insults of those who insult thee have fallen on me.

Psalm 69:9

In a sea of religious mediocrity, ardent faith stands out as a lone volcanic island. The seas wash its banks and try to erode its shores. But however vast the sea, it is no match for the inner fires that explode towards heaven.

PRAYER: O God, I want to develop the passionate spirit that you revealed in Jesus, rich in bold faith and adventurous trust. I want my life to become intense through faith, not flaccid through laziness. *Amen.*

143.
"Vinegar to Drink"

Read Psalm 69:16–21

> Thou knowest my reproach,
> and my shame and my dishonor;
> my foes are all known to thee.
> . . . .
> They gave me poison for food,
> and for my thirst they gave me vinegar to drink.
>> *Psalm 69:19, 21*

The terrors, the rejection, the humiliation and the pain that are threaded through this psalm were experienced most intensely by Jesus Christ. The Calvary crucifixion is the proper exposition and commentary for Psalm 69.

PRAYER: "O mysterious condescending! O abandonment sublime! Very God Himself is bearing all the suffering of time! Evermore for human failure by His passion we can plead; God has born all mortal anguish, surely He will know our need." *Amen.*

(W. J. Sparrow Simpson, "Cross of Jesus, Cross of Sorrow")

144.
"Pour Out Thy Indignation"

Read Psalm 69:22–29

> Pour out thy indignation upon them,
> and let thy burning anger overtake them.
>> *Psalm 69:24*

The curses preserved here are evidence that God listens to us when we are angry and accepts us even while we are burning with revenge. But they are not evidence that he does what we ask. God shows us how to respond to persecution in Jesus who prayed: "Father, forgive them, for they know not what they do" (Luke 23:24).

PRAYER: Dear God, teach me to love my enemies and do good to those who hate me, to bless those who curse me and pray for those who abuse me, to be merciful even as you, Father, are merciful, after the example of Jesus Christ. *Amen.*

145.
"Let Your Hearts Revive"

Read Psalm 69:30–36

Let the oppressed see it and be glad;
you who seek God, let your hearts revive.
Psalm 69:32

The great songs of praise are sung by those who have known the intensity of pain, the desperation of doubt, and the abyss of rejection. To all such persons, God's salvation and love are experienced as rescue and resurrection.

PRAYER: I praise you, merciful Father, that you have not led me in a way bound by grim duty and joyless servitude, but in one that, though it traverses "the valley of the shadow," always leads to "the house of the Lord." *Amen.*

(Ps. 23:4, 6)

146.
"Do Not Tarry!"

Read Psalm 70

But I am poor and needy;
hasten to me, O God!
Thou art my help and my deliverer;
O LORD, do not tarry!
Psalm 70:5

Prayer breaks through the lethargies of spirit that would put off eternal things until eternity. It introduces a note of urgency and crisis into the routines of the day. It is important *now, today,* that things be made right with God.

PRAYER: Come Lord Jesus! I want to know the fullness of your salvation now. I give myself completely to your love. I want my entire mind and my whole will at your disposal today. Come quickly, Lord Jesus, to my waiting spirit. *Amen.*

147.
"The Time of Old Age"

Read Psalm 71:1–16

Do not cast me off in the time of old age;
forsake me not when my strength is spent.
Psalm 71:9

Old age is a time of special need. This prayer expresses the foreboding that when strength fails and usefulness diminishes, life itself will lose its meaning. But God does not love us for what we can do for him, or for our usefulness to society, but for what we are.

PRAYER: Almighty God, help me to find the meaning of my life, not in the size of my paycheck nor in the list of things I can accomplish, but in the eternal purposes you have set for me in Jesus Christ, in whose name I pray. *Amen.*

148.
"To Old Age and Gray Hairs"

Read Psalm 71:17–24

So even to old age and gray hairs,
O God, do not forsake me,
till I proclaim thy might
to all the generations to come.
Thy power and thy righteousness, O God,
reach the high heavens.
Psalm 71:18

A long life accumulates material for praise. A vigorous youth and a reflective old age give bounds to a mass of evidence showing God's faithfulness and righteousness—all of which can be turned to the composition of convincing songs of gratitude.

PRAYER: As the days and years add up in me, O Lord, help me to grow in gratitude. As I grow older, give me a good memory for your acts of guidance and deliverance and a ready tongue for witness and praise. *Amen.*

149.
"Righteousness to the Royal Son!"

Read Psalm 72:1-7

> Give the king thy justice, O God,
> and thy righteousness to the royal son!
> *Psalm 72:1*

This prayer of intercession for the ruler is clearsighted in its perception of what is essential in government; justice for the poor, defense for the weak, deliverance for the needy.

PRAYER: O God, rule the nations of the earth: "May righteousness flourish, and peace abound" among the peoples. Use those in positions of power to nurture justice and accomplish peace, in the name of Jesus. *Amen.*

(Ps. 72:7)

150.
"May He Have Dominion"

Read Psalm 72:8-14

> May he have dominion from sea to sea,
> and from the River to the ends of the earth!
> *Psalm 72:8*

When we pray, "Thy kingdom come, Thy will be done, on earth as it is in heaven" (Matt. 7:10), we are looking for and participating in the complete establishment of what is only hinted at in human government, even at its best. All rule and all government are fulfilled, finally, in Jesus Christ.

PRAYER: "Blessing and honor and glory and power, wisdom and riches and strength evermore, give ye to Him who our battle hath won, whose are the Kingdom, the crown, and the throne." *Amen.*

(Horatius Bonar, "Blessing and Honor")

151.
"Amen and Amen!"

Read Psalm 72:15–20

Blessed be his glorious name for ever;
may his glory fill the whole earth! Amen and Amen!
Psalm 72:19

The double Amen is the emphatic, positive conclusion to these prayers. *Amen* is the Hebrew word for "yes," a "yes" that comes to its richest meaning in an affirmative response to God. We say yes to the God who says yes to us in Jesus Christ.

PRAYER: "Praise ye the Lord! O let all that is in me adore Him! All that hath life and breath, come now with praises before Him! Let the Amen sound from His people again: gladly for aye we adore Him." *Amen.*

(Joachim Neander, "Praise to the Lord, the Almighty,"
trans. by Catherine Winkworth)

152.
"Envious of the Arrogant"

Read Psalm 73:1–9

But as for me, my feet had almost stumbled,
my steps had well nigh slipped.
For I was envious of the arrogant,
When I saw the prosperity of the wicked.
Psalm 73:2–3

The appearance of prosperity in the wicked sets off an interior dialogue: if wicked people prosper and good people suffer, why be good? The question is boldly put to God by bewildered and discouraged men and women in and out of Scripture.

PRAYER: Almighty God, I keep demanding fairness, forgetting that in Jesus the best this world ever knew suffered the worst it could plot. Lead me to the maturity that finds eternal life, not in hand-outs or prizes, but in sharing your life in Jesus Christ. *Amen.*

153.
"Until I Went into the Sanctuary"

Read Psalm 73:10–20

> But when I thought how to understand this,
> it seemed to me a wearisome task,
> until I went into the sanctuary of God;
> then I perceived their end.
>
> *Psalm 73:16–17*

Verse 17 is the fulcrum for the psalm: "until" picks up the first sixteen verses of outraged sensitivity, of battered reason, of provoked faith, and marches them all into the sanctuary. When they emerge in the next verse (18), the once gaunt skeletons of troubled righteousness are clothed in robes of eternity. They are no longer troubles, but truths of cheer and hope.

PRAYER: Instead of wildly asking questions or clamorously making complaints, I ask you to lead me, Father, into acts of worship in which I will see creation whole and redemption complete, in Jesus' name. *Amen.*

154.
"It Is Good to Be Near God"

Read Psalm 73:21–28

> But for me it is good to be near God;
> I have made the Lord GOD my refuge,
> that I may tell of all thy works.
>
> *Psalm 73:28*

The psalmist evaluates the entire pilgrimage from faith to doubt and back to faith. The new faith sees the former doubt as brutish. And now, in spite of his bitter talk and little faith, he realizes that God has never left his side.

PRAYER: "In sweet communion, Lord, with Thee I constantly abide; my hand Thou holdest in Thy own to keep me near Thy side. . . . Whom have I, Lord, in heaven but Thee, to whom my thoughts aspire? And, having Thee, on earth is nought that I can yet desire." *Amen.*

("In Sweet Communion, Lord, with Thee," *The Psalter*, 1912)

155.
"Thy Foes Have Roared"

Read Psalm 74:1–11

> Thy foes have roared in the midst of thy holy place;
> they set up their own signs for signs.
>
> *Psalm 74:4*

The experience of catastrophe sets off a prayer of intercession: the intercessor feels the effects of sin, the destroying powers of evil, and the necessity for God's help. No hope of recovery seems likely unless God comes.

PRAYER: Almighty God, I place my concerns before you. The forces of evil seem overwhelming. Still, I know your power is mightier by far. Help me to direct my questions and my anxieties, my fears and my despair to you, in whom all victories will be accomplished. *Amen.*

156.
"Thou Didst Break the Heads of the Dragons"

Read Psalm 74:12–23

> Yet God my King is from of old,
> working salvation in the midst of the earth.
> Thou didst divide the sea by thy might;
> thou didst break the heads of the dragons on the waters.
>
> *Psalm 74:12–13*

That which is wrong and that which is evil God destroys. But he does it in order to save. As a bulldozer razes a slum tenement so that light-filled living quarters can be built, so God attacks chaos and wickedness in order to build a new heaven and a new earth.

PRAYER: Lord God of hosts, set my experience of present trouble firmly in the structure of your great acts of salvation. And then help me to believe that your way is being worked out even in the chaos of this world I live in, through Jesus Christ. *Amen.*

157.
"A Cup, with Foaming Wine"

Read Psalm 75

For in the hand of the Lord there is a cup,
with foaming wine, well mixed;
and he will pour a draught from it,
and all the wicked of the earth
shall drain it down to the dregs.
Psalm 75:8

The cup of foaming wine, destined for the wicked and predicted for centuries by prophet and psalmist, is finally grasped firmly by Jesus and drained to the dregs. When the deserved wrath of God is drunk by the undeserving Son of God, the cup of wrath becomes a cup of salvation.

PRAYER: I will seek justice, O God, not in the acts of men and not in my own attempts at goodness, but in the deep exchanges of forgiveness and redemption that take place in Jesus Christ. Free me from self-promotion and self-justification to sing the praise of my Savior and Lord, Jesus Christ. *Amen.*

158.
"The Wrath of Men Shall Praise Thee"

Read Psalm 76

Surely the wrath of men shall praise thee;
the residue of wrath thou wilt gird upon thee.
Psalm 76:10

Nothing is lost in the divine economy. Even the chaos and waste of battle redounds to God's glory: "Surely the wrath of man shall praise thee." No instance of man's wrath seemed more wasteful than that which put Jesus on a cross. "But where sin abounded grace did much more abound" (Rom. 5:20, KJV).

PRAYER: "In the cross of Christ I glory, towering o'er the wrecks of time; all the light of sacred story gathers round its head sublime." *Amen.*

(John Bowring, "In the Cross of Christ I Glory")

159.
"I Think of God, and I Moan"

Read Psalm 77:1–10

I think of God, and I moan;
I meditate, and my spirit faints.
Psalm 77:3

Any place is the right place to begin prayer. Groaning, discomfort, and a speechless grief initiate this one. It is a troubled cry, a troubled meditation. Brash, even blasphemous, doubts and demands are not forbidden. But if we start out feeling sorry for ourselves, we must not be surprised if we end up in a place quite different.

PRAYER: I offer you, O Christ, all my unbelieving, unacceptable and unlovely feelings and thoughts. I will not hide them in a private sulk. Keep me, though, from wallowing in self-pity. Deliver me from despair and doubt, in the name of Jesus, "who in every respect has been tempted as we are, yet without sinning." *Amen.*

(Heb. 4:15)

160.
"I Will Call to Mind the Deeds of the Lord"

Read Psalm 77:11–20

I will call to mind the deeds of the LORD;
yea, I will remember thy wonders of old.
Psalm 77:11

Troubles exacerbated by self-pity are brought under the operations of grace. The spirit, rescued from morbid introspection, sees clouds pouring water, skies thundering, and arrows flashing—God is acting for men in need. The tiresome "I think of God and I moan" has, in the course of prayer, become the exhilarating "I will . . . muse on thy mighty deeds. . . . What god is great like our God?"

PRAYER: O God of Exodus and Easter, I remember all I know of your love poured out in deliverance and resurrection. You rescue from sin and you raise to new life. You sustain and you lead. I praise you for your unending mercy and your untiring faithfulness. *Amen.*

161.
"Tell to the Coming Generation"

Read Psalm 78:1–8

We will not hide them from their children,
but tell to the coming generation
the glorious deeds of the LORD, and his might,
and the wonders which he has wrought.
Psalm 78:4

Everyone who experiences God's grace has an obligation to pass on what he knows. It is not necessary that each new Christian start from scratch learning the way of faith by trial and error. God's people have a history, an accumulation of experience useful for instruction and inspiration. Only the man who ignores history is condemned to repeat it.

PRAYER: God, I thank you for the story of how you have loved and led your people, the ways you have disciplined and delivered, the ways you have rescued and reconciled. Give me a desire to pass the story on, sharing its truths with friends and family. *Amen.*

162.
"They Forgot What He Had Done"

Read Psalm 78:9–31

They did not keep God's covenant,
but refused to walk according to his law.
They forgot what he had done,
and the miracles that he had shown them.
Psalm 78:9–10

History is of no use if we don't remember it. The rich heritage of God's mighty works gives neither insight nor inspiration if we are ignorant of it. The stories of God's guidance and preservation can, though, be put to the uses of trust and hope.

PRAYER: Cure me, Christ, of my amnesia. Put my memory to work in reflecting on all the ways you have saved and blessed. Imprint these memories on my mind so that no trial or pain will arrive unaccompanied by the expectation that you will guard and guide me. *Amen.*

163.
"Yet He, Being Compassionate"

Read Psalm 78:32–55

Yet he, being compassionate,
  forgave their iniquity,
  and did not destroy them;
he restrained his anger often,
  and did not stir up all his wrath.

Psalm 78:38

While some tally the sins of men and conclude that there is no hope for humanity, others are noticing that the grace of Christ is even more evident—establishing salvation, developing reconciliation, and building the Kingdom of God.

PRAYER: I will not be disheartened, O God, by those who tell me stories of man's decadence and society's disintegration; I have heard those stories before. Instead I will see every sin as a place where your forgiveness can operate and every rebellion as a focus for your redemption. You are more than a match for sin—mine and everyone's. *Amen.*

164.
"Guided Them with Skilful Hand"

Read Psalm 78:56–72

He chose David his servant,
  and took him from the sheepfolds;
from tending the ewes that had young he brought him
  to be the shepherd of Jacob his people,
  of Israel his inheritance.
With upright heart he tended them,
  and guided them with skilful hand.

Psalm 78:70–72

David, more than any other leader in Israel, exhibited the twin qualities of strength and gentleness which are characteristic both of good shepherds and of the God who revealed himself in Jesus Christ.

PRAYER: "Guide me, O Thou great Jehovah, pilgrim through this barren land; I am weak, but Thou art mighty; hold me with Thy powerful hand; Bread of heaven, feed me till I want no more." *Amen.*

(William Williams, "Guide Me, O Thou Great Jehovah,"
trans. by Peter Williams)

165.
"We Have Become a Taunt"

> We have become a taunt to our neighbors,
> mocked and derided by those round about us.
> *Psalm 79:4*

The desecration of Jerusalem by the Babylonians is behind this prayer. Their ruthless pillage accounts for the shouts for vengeance. But beside the desire for revenge there is an awareness that God is at work in judgment, and that accounts for the repentant cries for compassion.

PRAYER: O God, help me to be aware of the wrongs done to your children, to be sensitive to the violence done to your people. Then teach me to pray in a caring, compassionate spirit for your justice and your salvation. *Amen.*

166.
"Let Thy Face Shine"

Read Psalm 80:1–7

> Restore us, O God;
> let thy face shine, that we may be saved!
> *Psalm 80:3*

From Genesis, where "Let there be light" (1:3) is the first recorded sentence of God, to Revelation, which concludes, "They shall see his face. . . . And night shall be no more; they need no light of lamp or sun, for the Lord God will be their light" (22:4–5), the Scriptures tell of God's acts under the image of light, his shining forth in creation and redemption.

PRAYER: "Light of light, enlighten me, now anew the day is dawning; sun of grace, the shadows flee; brighten Thou my Sabbath morning; with Thy joyous sunshine blest, happy is my day of rest." *Amen.*

(Benjamin Schmolck, "Light of Light, Enlighten Me,"
trans. by Catherine Winkworth)

93

167.
"Have Regard for This Vine"

Read Psalm 80:8–19

> Turn again, O God of hosts!
> Look down from heaven, and see;
> have regard for this vine,
> the stock which thy right hand planted.
> *Psalm 80:14–15*

God's people are not fragile flowers that can be withered in a day by a merciless sun or destroyed in a moment by a careless boot. We are a vine—tough, tenacious, planted by God and, despite ravages of persecution and judgment, brought to final fruition in Jesus who said, "I am the vine, you are the branches" (John 15:5).

PRAYER: Enter my present trouble, God of strength and compassion. Protect me from despair and from faintheartedness. Encourage me with hope. Make me strong in Christ, "the man of thy right hand." *Amen.*

(Ps. 80:17)

168.
"Open Your Mouth Wide"

Read Psalm 81

> I am the LORD your God,
> who brought you up out of the land of Egypt.
> Open your mouth wide, and I will fill it.
> *Psalm 81:10*

Perpetual festival is God's will for his people. If our common lives don't come up to that standard, the fault is not in the promises or intent of God but simply because "Israel would have none of me" (v. 11).

PRAYER: I haven't asked enough from you, O God—I see that now. Remembering what you have promised and what you have done, I will rejoice in festival celebration, taking what you so generously give and sharing what you so joyously provide. In Jesus Christ. *Amen.*

169.
"Give Justice to the Weak"

Read Psalm 82

Give justice to the weak and the fatherless;
  maintain the right of the afflicted and the destitute.
Rescue the weak and the needy;
  deliver them from the hand of the wicked.

Psalm 82:3–4

God, the judge of all the earth, delegates his judicial authority to men, but they not infrequently abuse it. Judges who do not learn their jurisprudence from a just God trample the needy instead of defending them and exploit them instead of delivering them.

PRAYER: "Tie in a living tether the prince and priest and thrall, bind all our lives together, smite us and save us all; in ire and exultation aflame with faith, and free, lift up a living nation, a single sword to Thee." *Amen.*

(G. K. Chesterton, "O God of Earth and Altar")

170.
"Do Not Keep Silence"

Read Psalm 83

O God, do not keep silence;
  do not hold thy peace or be still, O God!
For lo, thy enemies are in tumult;
  those who hate thee have raised their heads.

Psalm 83:1–2

History is noisy with the activity of conspirators against God: "thy enemies are in tumult" (v. 2). The conspicuous great of the earth—Edom, Philistia, Assyria—fill the air with an arrogant din that cancels out meaning. "So few of the Big ever listen" (W. H. Auden, *Homage to Clio*, p. 5). Meanwhile prayer approaches the (supposed) silence of God and hears quiet words that fill life with significant hope.

PRAYER: I enter the place of prayer, dear God, to listen to what you have to say. I have been shouted at, accused and threatened from newspaper, radio and television. Now I want to hear the syllables of hope that come in the still small voice of your Spirit and establish you as Lord in my heart as well as "Most High over all the earth." *Amen.*

(Ps. 83:18)

171.
"Strength to Strength"

Read Psalm 84:1–7

> Blessed are the men whose strength is in thee,
>   in whose heart are the highways to Zion.
> As they go through the valley of Baca
>   they make it a place of springs;
>   the early rain also covers it with pools.
> They go from strength to strength.
>
> *Psalm 84:5–7*

The act of worship internalizes the way of discipleship into habits of praise and obedience so that life is not a depressing descent into senility but an exhilarating ascent to strength.

PRAYER: I lift my eyes to you, O God, in worship and adoration. I focus on your promises and expect your grace. I gather all my needs and desires and bring them to you in the name of Jesus Christ. *Amen.*

172.
"A Day in Thy Courts"

Read Psalm 84:8–12

> For a day in thy courts is better
>   than a thousand elsewhere.
> I would rather be a doorkeeper in the house of my God
>   than dwell in the tents of wickedness.
>
> *Psalm 84:10*

The sanctuary—the place where God's people meet to sing praises, to renew covenant obedience, to be instructed in God's word—is filled with the best of associations. The concentration of memory and meaning that takes place there makes it more desirable than any other place.

PRAYER: Lord God, you are sun and shield: the light of your word gives meaning to what I experience, the strength of your presence provides protection against despair. I thank you for hours of worship when I can listen again to that word and reaffirm that presence, even in Jesus Christ. *Amen.*

173.
"Revive Us Again"

Read Psalm 85:1–7

Wilt thou not revive us again,
    that thy people may rejoice in thee?
Show us thy steadfast love, O LORD,
    and grant us thy salvation.
                    Psalm 85:6–7

Nothing suffers from time quite so much as religion. The skeletal structure of obedience becomes arthritic and the circulatory system of praise becomes sluggish. The prayer "revive us again" keeps the body of Christ youthful and responsive to every new mercy and grace in God.

PRAYER: O God, when my faith gets overladen with dust, blow it clean with the wind of your Spirit. When my habits of obedience get stiff and rusty, anoint them with the oil of your Spirit. Restore the enthusiasm of my first love for you and the alacrity of my first obedience to you, in Jesus' name. *Amen.*

174.
"Righteousness and Peace Will Kiss"

Read Psalm 85:8–13

Steadfast love and faithfulness will meet;
    righteousness and peace will kiss each other.
                    Psalm 85:10

The great attributes of God (steadfast love, faithfulness, righteousness, peace), thinned by our faint imaginations into bloodless abstractions, are given personal vitality by acts of God: "And the Word became flesh and dwelt among us, full of grace and truth; we have beheld his glory" (John 1:14).

PRAYER: I want, O God, every truth you announce to become an experience in which I am conscious of meeting another in love and touching another in compassion, even as you met and touched so many in Jesus Christ, in whose name I pray. *Amen.*

175.
"Unite My Heart to Fear Thy Name"

Read Psalm 86

> Teach me thy way, O LORD,
> that I may walk in thy truth;
> unite my heart to fear thy name.
>
> *Psalm 86:11*

There are fifteen petitions in these seventeen verses: concentration is weakened by the distraction of clamoring needs. Then a single petition weaves all needs into one prayer: "Unite my heart to fear thy name." As a harpoon has many barbs but one point, so this prayer has many petitions but a single thrust.

PRAYER: God, my soul feels scattered and incoherent like that poor wretch Legion ("for we are many"). Gather up my diverse needs, my conflicting desires, my jumbled identity, and make a harmonious whole of me, "unite my heart to fear thy name." *Amen.*

(Mark 5:2–10)

176.
"All My Springs Are in You"

Read Psalm 87

> And of Zion it shall be said,
> "This one and that one were born in her"; . . .
> . . . .
> Singers and dancers alike say,
> "All my springs are in you."
>
> *Psalm 87:5, 7*

New birth is the experience of finding one's origin and identity in the acts of God instead of in the acts of parents. Creation, not copulation, marks our beginning. We are much more apt to find out who we are in a place of worship than by examining a birth certificate or citizenship paper.

PRAYER: I celebrate my origins in you, O God. You fashioned me in love and destined me to eternal life. In all my words and acts may I reflect that love and demonstrate that life, both enjoying and glorifying your name, according to your plan in Jesus Christ. *Amen.*

177.
"Like One Forsaken"

Read Psalm 88

I am reckoned among those who go down to the Pit;
I am a man who has no strength,
like one forsaken among the dead,
  like the slain that lie in the grave,
like those whom thou dost remember no more,
  for they are cut off from thy hand.
Psalm 88:4–5

Two images describe the misery: that of being buried alive ("thou hast put me in the depths of the Pit") and that of drowning ("thou dost overwhelm me with all thy waves"). The grave, whether in cold earth or deep waters, tells the story of extreme trouble. In this time of need the name of God is repeated four times (vv. 1, 9, 13, 14): no trouble can rob us of the power to pray.

PRAYER: Dear Jesus, you were tested at every point that I can be. Lead me through the time of testing, defend me against despair and guide me into the place where my prayers for help will be changed into shouts of praise. *Amen.*

178.
"I Will Sing of Thy Steadfast Love"

Read Psalm 89:1–4

I will sing of thy steadfast love,
  O LORD, for ever;
with my mouth I will proclaim thy
  faithfulness to all generations.
Psalm 89:1

"Steadfast love" and "faithfulness"—God's relationship with his creation and his steadiness in his covenant—make a tune to sing. The two words are themes and provide the melodic structure upon which this moving song is constructed.

PRAYER: O God, within the sometimes puzzling experiences of this pilgrimage, I will gratefully sing of your steadfast love and your faithfulness which, despite my stuttering steps and recurrent doubt, steadily develop a redeeming purpose in my life. *Amen.*

179.
"The People Who Know the Festal Shout"
Read Psalm 89:5–18

Blessed are the people who know the festal shout,
who walk, O LORD, in the light of thy countenance,
Psalm 89:16

The word translated "festal shout" is a technical word meaning the learned response a congregation makes in worship—the ways in which the people celebrate God's acts of creation and redemption. Some parts of the spiritual life can only take place in private behind the closed door; other parts must be nurtured in the company of the gathered faithful in public worship.

PRAYER: Father, thank you for the ways of worship provided for me—the prayers and the hymns, the place and the people. Thank you for companions who "know the festal shout." Train me in alert praise and attentive listening. *Amen.*

180.
"I Will Not Lie to David"

Ps 89:34 ~ "My cov will not alter that's forth of my mouth."

Read Psalm 89:19–37

Once for all I have sworn by my holiness;
I will not lie to David.
Psalm 89:35

When there is change in our fortunes we think it is because God has changed his mind about us. Israel's mature witness is that there is no fickleness or inconsistency in God. There is much that we don't understand in God but nothing base or unworthy in him.

PRAYER: Thank you, Father, for the reassuring witness of the generations of believers that there is no hesitation in your will, no deceit in your promises, and no flaws in your covenant commitments. *Amen.*

181.
"Cast Off and Rejected"

Read Psalm 89:38–48

But now thou hast cast off and rejected,
thou art full of wrath against thy anointed.
Psalm 89:38

Trust in God is tested by the tremors of judgment. No covenant precludes such experience and no faith is exempt from such testing. The marvel of the gospel is that faith emerges from such troubles with stronger song and firmer trust.

PRAYER: Take the incidents in my life, dear God, that I interpret as your rejection and disapproval and show me how they are consistent with your covenant love, used by your Spirit for my salvation. In Jesus' name. *Amen.*

182.
"Scorned . . . Blessed"

Read Psalm 89:49–52

Remember, O Lord, how thy servant is scorned;
how I bear in my bosom the insults of the peoples,. . .
. . . .
Blessed be the LORD for ever!
Amen and Amen.
Psalm 89:50, 52

The psalm as a whole is a study in proportions. The jagged intensity of the complaint (vv. 38–51) is set in an expansive witness to God's promise (vv. 1–37, 52). Thirteen verses of trouble are buttressed by thirty-nine verses of trust. Devotion offers both trust and trouble to the God who brings final blessing in Jesus Christ.

PRAYER: "So long Thy power hath blest me, sure it still will lead me on, o'er moor and fen, o'er crag and torrent, till the night is gone; and with the morn those angel faces smile, which I have loved long since, and lost awhile." *Amen.*

(John Henry Newman, "Lead Kindly Light")

183.
"Our Dwelling Place"

Read Psalm 90:1–2

Lord, thou hast been our dwelling place
in all generations.
Psalm 90:1

The metaphor of creation ("brought forth . . . formed") is from the language of childbirth. God is previous to the age-old mountains just as a father is previous to his sons. Refuge in such a God is not retreat to a makeshift shelter, but habitation in an eternal dwelling place.

PRAYER: "Before the hills in order stood, or earth received her frame, from everlasting Thou art God, to endless years the same. O God, our Help in ages past, our Hope for years to come, be Thou our Guard while life shall last, and our eternal Home." *Amen.*
(Isaac Watts, "O God, Our Help in Ages Past")

184.
"They Are Like a Dream"

Read Psalm 90:3–6

Thou dost sweep men away; they are like a dream,
like grass which is renewed in the morning:
in the morning it flourishes and is renewed;
in the evening it fades and withers.
Psalm 90:5–6

The comparison of man's brevity to God's eternity makes it clear that the only basis for existence, beyond fleeting sensations, is in God. Separated from God, man is like a dream separated from the sleeper—the most insubstantial condition imaginable. But joined to God, we are part of an eternal reality.

PRAYER: Forgive me, Father, when I try to take my few years, my meager strength and my uncertain ideas and try to make a life out of them. It is a shabby effort at best. I will, instead, turn it all over to you to make of it what you will, in Jesus Christ. *Amen.*

185.
"Consumed by Thy Anger"

Read Psalm 90:7–10

> For we are consumed by thy anger;
>   by thy wrath we are overwhelmed.
> Thou hast set our iniquities before thee,
>   our secret sins in the light of thy countenance.
> *Psalm 90:7–8*

"It often happened to me, when I was a monk," wrote Martin Luther, "that when reading this psalm I had to lay it aside. For I did not know at that time that these frightening truths were not intended by Moses for a terrified soul" (*Luther's Works*, 13:86). After his evangelical experience, though, it ceased to be a terror and became a comfort, and he wrote: "his wrath is a wrath of compassion."

PRAYER: Lord God, there is much unproductive stuff in my life that needs pruning: I submit myself willingly to your scrutiny. I know that your anger is only the other side of your love and that any pain I experience is only a part of my growth in your love. *Amen.*

186.
"So Teach Us to Number Our Days"

Read Psalm 90:11–12

> So teach us to number our days
>   that we may get a heart of wisdom.
> *Psalm 90:12*

Every moment counts, not in the sense that we have to be constantly busy in order to prove our worth or make a mark in the world, but in the sense that all time is material which God uses to love us, guide us, correct us and redeem us. "Moses wants all of us to become such arithmeticians" (Martin Luther, *Luther's Works*, 13:128).

PRAYER: "Day by day, dear Lord, of thee three things I pray: to see Thee more clearly, love Thee more dearly, follow Thee more nearly, day by day." *Amen.*

(Richard of Chichester)

187.
"Make Us Glad"

Read Psalm 90:13–17

Make us glad as many days as thou hast afflicted us,
and as many years as we have seen evil.
Psalm 90:15

The slow burning fuse of meditation reaches the powder of prayer and detonates the explosive question: "How long?" Eight petitions are put before God. Then, as the petitions mature, there is rejoicing, gladness and a virile enthusiasm for work.

PRAYER: Not by increasing the tempo of my life, O Lord, or trying to add extra years to it, but by sinking the life that I have—this hour, this day—into your will and in your presence, may I find my hope and my blessing. *Amen.*

188.
"Under His Wing"

Read Psalm 91:1–6

He will cover you with his pinions,
and under his wings you will find refuge;
his faithfulness is a shield and buckler.
Psalm 91:4

Just as evil comes to us under various guises, so the experience of protection in God is experienced under a variety of forms. Whatever the danger, there is a matching deliverance. "In the world you have tribulation; but be of good cheer, I have overcome the world" (John 16:33).

PRAYER: I need your protective help, Almighty God: be to me a refuge and a fortress. Grant that I may be more expectant of your protective care than fearful of the dangers of evil. For Jesus' sake. *Amen.*

189.
"No Evil Shall Befall You"

Read Psalm 91:7–10

Because you have made the LORD your refuge,
the Most High your habitation,
no evil shall befall you,
no scourge come near your tent.
Psalm 91:9–10

All the water in the ocean cannot sink a ship unless it gets inside; and all the trouble in the world cannot harm us unless it gains entrance to our hearts. On such analogy, faith is pitch and caulking. Jesus prayed: "I do not pray that thou shouldst take them out of the world, but that thou shouldst keep them from the evil one" (John 17:15).

PRAYER: I know, great God, that no tribulations I face can separate me from your love, and no evil I encounter can confuse your purposes in me. I thank you for your victory in Jesus Christ. *Amen.*

190.
"His Angels"

Read Psalm 91:11–13

For he will give his angels charge of you
to guard you in all your ways.
Psalm 91:11

Angels are the messengers of God who carry out his will among men. They are the reality of God active in the details of human existence. Angels are specific, particular manifestations of God's providence in the world of our daily affairs.

PRAYER: I submit myself to your care, merciful Father. I will find in the provisions of this day the evidence of your love for me and the experience of your care for me. *Amen.*

191.
"Because He Cleaves to Me in Love"

Read Psalm 91:14–16

Because he cleaves to me in love, I will deliver him;
I will protect him, because he knows my name.
Psalm 91:14

All that is prayed for and believed is confirmed in the action of God. God enters our lives and acts in ways that meet every need. Blessings are exchanged.

PRAYER: I do cleave to you, O God, in love. And I do need all that you can do for me: deliver, protect, rescue, honor and save. Thank you for the richness of your promise and the steadfastness in your performance, even in Jesus Christ. *Amen.*

192.
"It Is Good to Give Thanks"

Read Psalm 92:1–4

It is good to give thanks to the LORD,
to sing praises to thy name, O Most High.
Psalm 92:1

Thanks to God is not a grudging act of courtesy, but an exuberant explosion of delight. It is not the polite exchange of amenities, but the songburst of joy. Every day provides new opportunities and fresh forms in which to proclaim praise.

PRAYER: Dear God, I will greet morning as a rising of the light of your love upon me; I will kneel at evening and receive your benediction. In between I will use every tune I know to carry a song of praise to you. *Amen.*

193.
"Thy Thoughts Are Very Deep"

Read Psalm 92:5–11

How great are thy works, O LORD!
Thy thoughts are very deep!
Psalm 92:5

There is a kind of dullness which is oblivious to both sure causes and certain consequences. But he who has his eyes open quickly sees evidence of God on all sides. Intelligent observation turns up ever new materials for praise. "I greet him the days I meet him, and bless when I understand" (Gerard Manley Hopkins, "The Wreck of the Deutschland").

PRAYER: Give me a quickness of mind to see your hand in all things, O God—your gracious acts in creation and your steady purposes in redemption. I do not want to be among those who grope in the dark but with those who walk in your light. *Amen.*

194.
"Ever Full of Sap and Green"

Read Psalm 92:12–15

[The righteous] still bring forth fruit in old age,
they are ever full of sap and green.
Psalm 92:14

The life of faith does not deteriorate or wear out. The longer we praise God, the more vigorous we become. There is a flourishing of faith which properly comes to its most lively expression in the later years.

PRAYER: O God, as I receive new energy each day from you, may there be juices of love and hope flowing through my veins, bringing fruits of righteousness to my praising and my loving, through Jesus Christ. *Amen.*

195.
"The Lord Reigns"

Read Psalm 93

The LORD reigns; he is robed in majesty;
the LORD is robed, he is girded with strength.
Yea, the world is established; it shall never be moved.
Psalm 93:1

The rule of God is beyond challenge. The most terrible assault imaginable to the ancient Hebrew mind, the raging of the sea, cannot touch the Lord in his majesty. If we can be sure about the solidity of his rule, we can also be sure of his decrees. What he *says* is as sure as what he *is*.

PRAYER: "God, the Lord, a King remaineth, robed in His own glorious light; God hath robed Himself and reigneth; He hath girt Himself with might. Alleluia! Alleluia! God is King in depth and height! God is King in depth and height!" *Amen.*

(John Keble, "God, the Lord, a King Remaineth")

196.
"Fools, When Will You Be Wise?"

Read Psalm 94:1–11

Understand, O dullest of the people!
Fools, when will you be wise?
Psalm 94:8

It is customary to attribute a canny intelligence to those who get rich by deceiving others or who get power by propagating falsehoods. But the man of God sees in them, not sharpness of mind, but dullness of spirit; not mental dexterity, but moral clumsiness. Moral laws work, if less visibly, even more inexorably than physical laws.

PRAYER: O God, act in righteous judgment now. Put down the arrogant and lift up the humble. Make me a participant in the working out of your justice among all who are hurt or despised or degraded. In the name of Jesus, who promised to bless the poor in spirit. *Amen.*

197.
"The Man Whom Thou Dost Chasten"
Read Psalm 94:12–15

Blessed is the man whom thou dost chasten, O LORD,
and whom thou dost teach out of thy law.
Psalm 94:12

If God hated us he would punish us; if he were indifferent to us
he would ignore us. But he loves us. One of the ways he expresses
his love is through chastening—the disciplined training that shapes
our lives out of evil ways into righteous acts.

PRAYER: Father, I receive your words of correction and your acts
of discipline. Help me to learn obedience through the things that I
suffer, even as Jesus did. *Amen.*

198.
"Thy Consolations Cheer My Soul"
Read Psalm 94:16–23

When the cares of my heart are many,
thy consolations cheer my soul.
Psalm 94:19

No matter how perilous life seems in a world ruled by the wicked
("my foot slips"), no matter how vulnerable our anxieties make us
("the cares of my heart"), God has power to dissolve the cares and
dissipate the perils. God's consolations penetrate the deepest re-
cesses of body and soul and bring an inner health that breaks out in
confident cheer.

PRAYER: I need your consolations, O God, so that I will see my life
held together by the one who created this world and is redeeming it,
not victimized by those who "frame mischief by statute" and walk
over anyone who is poorer or weaker than they. Make me strong in
Jesus Christ. *Amen.*

(Ps. 94:20)

199.
"Let Us Make a Joyful Noise"

Read Psalm 95:1–5

O come, let us sing to the LORD;
let us make a joyful noise to the rock of our salvation!
Psalm 95:1

God is the reason for worship. The awesome power of God makes it sure that we shall worship; the graciousness of his will makes it certain that our worship shall be glad.

PRAYER: I praise your great name, O God. Every song I sing of your power and love, of your grace and glory, discovers fresh reasons for singing another. All praise to Father, Son, and Holy Spirit. *Amen.*

200.
"Meribah ... Massah"

Read Psalm 95:6–11

O that day you would hearken to his voice!
Harden not your hearts, as at Meribah,
as on the day at Massah in the wilderness.
Psalm 95:7–8

The opposite of worship is wandering. The alternatives to the "Let us worship and bow down," in which we give our attention to God's love and direction, are strife (Meribah) and temptation (Massah), in which we look out for ourselves and snatch what we can in a trackless desert.

PRAYER: Father, I will give my attention to you in faithful worship, listening to your words of truth and guidance; and I will put aside the contentious scrabbling for my own way, which only adds years of wandering in the wilderness of my sins. In Jesus' name. *Amen.*

201.
"A New Song"

Read Psalm 96

O sing to the LORD a new song;
sing to the LORD, all the earth!
Psalm 96:1

The vigorous and varied praise of the "new song" has its cause in the proclamation, "The Lord reigns!" (v. 10). When we discover God's rule, the ways in which he extends his lordship in grace and mercy, our vocabulary of praise expands markedly.

PRAYER: How glorious to be ruled by you, O Lord, and not by the abstract, mechanical laws of nature or the capricious, uncertain laws of society. Rule me in the person of Jesus Christ, in whom your kingdom is even now present. *Amen.*

202.
"His Lightnings Lighten the World"

Read Psalm 97:1–9

The LORD reigns; let the earth rejoice;
let the many coastlands be glad!
· ·
His lightnings lighten the world;
the earth sees and trembles.
Psalm 97:1, 4

The memory of Sinai evokes praise. At Sinai God's people realized God's rule in deliverance (out of Egypt) and in guidance (the Ten Commandments). God's rule was personal experience, not a legal or political abstraction, as Israel lived as a redeemed people (no longer in Egypt) and as a guided people (bound to the covenant).

PRAYER: God, your word is powerful, delivering me from despair; your word is wise, guiding me through uncertainty. I am able to leave sin and travel towards righteousness. Thank you for your deliverance and your guidance. *Amen.*

203.
"Joy for the Upright"

Read Psalm 97:10–12

Light dawns for the righteous,
and joy for the upright in heart.
Psalm 97:11

Living under God's rule enables us not only to complete his will, but to fulfill our own. We find wholeness in becoming what we were intended in creation. The wholeness feels good: we know joy and therefore rejoice.

PRAYER: "Rivers to the ocean run, nor stay in all their course; fire ascending seeks the sun; both speed them to their source; so my soul, derived from God, longs to view His glorious face, forward tends to His abode, to rest in His embrace." *Amen.*

(Robert Seagrave, "Rise, My Soul, and Stretch Thy Wings")

204.
"Let the Sea Roar"

Read Psalm 98

Let the sea roar, and all that fills it;
the world and those who dwell in it!
Psalm 98:7

Salvation, which brings God's wholeness into our lives, develops a capacity in us for total response, which is praise. Everything and everyone is enlisted in the work of praise: the songs of the people, the melodies of musical instruments, and the sounds of nature.

PRAYER: My God and King, bird song and sea-roar accompany the praise I lift to you. Mine is no solitary voice raised in gratitude; there is a thunderous and multitudinous congregation making sounds of thanksgiving, and I am glad to be a part of it. *Amen.*

205.
"Holy Is He!"

Read Psalm 99

The LORD is great in Zion;
  he is exalted over all the peoples.
Let them praise thy great and terrible name!
Holy is he!
Psalm 99:2–3

Holiness is the quality in God that cares about our sin and the capacity in him to do something about it. When sinners worship gods of their making, they drag the gods down to their level. When sinners worship a God of holiness, they are lifted to his level.

PRAYER: "Holy, Holy, Holy! Though the darkness hide Thee, though the eye of sinful man Thy glory may not see, only Thou art holy; there is none beside Thee perfect in power, in love, and purity." *Amen.*

(Reginald Heber, "Holy, Holy, Holy, Lord God Almighty")

206.
"Serve the Lord with Gladness!"

Read Psalm 100

Serve the LORD with gladness!
Come into his presence with singing!
Psalm 100:2

Eight different words urge praise to God. The similarity of the eight words marks the dominance of praise; the dissimilarity indicates its complex, many-sided nature. Praise is no dull routine to be tossed off in sluggish monosyllables; it is a happy, creative imagination that is aware of God.

PRAYER: "All people that on earth do dwell, sing to the Lord with cheerful voice; Him serve with mirth, His praise forth tell, come ye before Him and rejoice." *Amen.*

(William Kethe, "All People That on Earth Do Dwell")

207.
"I Will Sing of Loyalty and of Justice"

Read Psalm 101

I will sing of loyalty and of justice;
to thee, O LORD, I will sing.
Psalm 101:1

The Christian who sings of moral conviction and loyal determination in personal (vv. 1–4) and professional (vv. 5–8) relationships finds that the song puts steel into every resolve to do a difficult job well to the glory of God.

PRAYER: Father, you have given me work to do: give me also the ethical stamina to do it right. No work will be a burden as long as I know I am sharing your will; no task will be demeaning when I know that I am participating in your ways. For Jesus' sake. *Amen.*

208.
"Like an Owl of the Waste Places"

Read Psalm 102:1–17

I am like a vulture of the wilderness,
like an owl of the waste places;
I lie awake,
I am like a lonely bird on the housetop.
Psalm 102:6–7

Sin does terrible things to us: it cuts us off from experiences of intimacy, driving us into positions of isolation where we are enclosed in self-pity and a withering preoccupation with the self. The vulture and the owl, solitary and predatory, are similes for the soul sunk in sin.

PRAYER: There is nothing worse than feeling separated from you, Father—no pain more hurting, no desolation more desperate. At the places where my sin has turned me in upon myself expand me outwards in faith to receive forgiveness and engage in praise. *Amen.*

209.
"A People Yet Unborn May Praise"
Read Psalm 102:18–22

> Let this be recorded for a generation to come,
> so that a people yet unborn may praise the LORD.
> *Psalm 102:18*

The gloomy "man is born to trouble as the sparks fly upward" (Job 5:7) is countered by this glorious "a people yet unborn may praise the Lord." If pain and sorrow are certain, praise and salvation are even more so. If the results of sin are inevitable, the consequences of grace are irresistible.

PRAYER: Lord God, I survey the ruins around me—broken promises, plotted malice, failed love—and I am brought low. Then I review the expectations of faith—the visitation of your spirit, the deliverance by Messiah, the praising worship of the redeemed—and I am lifted up. *Amen.*

210.
"Thou Art the Same"
Read Psalm 102:23–28

> [The heavens and the earth] will perish, but thou dost endure;
> they will all wear out like a garment.
> Thou changest them like raiment, and they pass away;
> but thou art the same, and thy years have no end.
> *Psalm 102:26–27*

All life is unfinished. Nothing we do is complete in itself. Only by becoming part of the work of God do we find a proper beginning and a satisfying ending to our existence. When we participate in the great themes and continuities of God himself, our lives make sense.

PRAYER: Take, Lord, all my parts—whatever years and whatever acts you can salvage out of my sin—and build a new life. Lay foundations of eternity in me; construct spacious stretches of salvation around me. In Jesus' name. *Amen.*

211.
"Forget Not All His Benefits"

Read Psalm 103:1–5

Bless the LORD, O my soul,
and forget not all his benefits.
Psalm 103:2

Forgetfulness atrophies the muscles of praise and leaves them flabby and passive. Remembrance internalizes a history of grace and strengthens praise into blessing, so that we act in a renewing way on our environment.

PRAYER: What blessings I have experienced! What benefits I have been given! I will compile my own list of goodness through the hours of this day and give you praise, O God, for each item. Stir my memory and quicken my tongue, for Jesus' sake. *Amen.*

212.
"As Far as the East Is from the West"

Read Psalm 103:6–18

As far as the east is from the west,
so far does he remove our transgressions from us.
Psalm 103:12

The experience of forgiveness provokes the activity of praise. In forgiveness our sins are personally confronted, not impersonally condemned. We experience God's severity, but even more his grace.

PRAYER: Merciful Father, I used to try to hide my true self from you, assuming that if you knew all about me you would necessarily condemn me. Now I know that your knowledge is gracious and that deception is futile. Come to me with just the right mixture of severity and kindness. Judge me and save me, both at the same time, in Jesus Christ. *Amen.*

213.
"Bless the Lord, O My Soul!"

Read Psalm 103:19–22

> Bless the LORD, all his works,
> in all places of his dominion.
> Bless the LORD, O my soul!
> *Psalm 103:22*

This is one of the "finest blossoms on the tree of biblical faith" (Artur Weiser, *The Psalms*, p. 657). It is balanced, intense and inclusive. The people's tradition and the individual's experience are integrated in praise. Adoration is at both center and periphery.

PRAYER: "Bless, O my soul! the living God; call home thy thoughts that rove abroad; let all the powers within me join in work and worship so divine. Bless, O my soul! the God of grace; His favors claim thy highest praise; why should the wonders He hath wrought be lost in silence and forgot?" *Amen.*

(Isaac Watts, "Bless, O My Soul! The Living God")

214.
"The Winds Thy Messengers"

Read Psalm 104:1–4

> Bless the LORD, O my soul!
> O LORD my God, thou art very great!
> Thou art clothed with honor and majesty,
> . . . .
> who makest the winds thy messengers,
> fire and flame thy ministers.
> *Psalm 104:1, 4*

Significantly, there are no "nature psalms" in the Bible, only "Creator psalms"—passages which develop a rich vocabulary of praise to God out of the stuff of his creation. Observations on the visible world become elements of adoration to the invisible maker.

PRAYER: Like the wind, O God, you are invisible; yet all your effects are visible—from the gentle breeze that cools and comforts to the roaring hurricane that moves and rearranges. I ready myself to respond to every aspect of your creative work in me: "Breathe on me, breath of God." *Amen.*

(Edwin Hatch)

215.
"Thou Didst Set a Bound"

Read Psalm 104:5–9

Thou didst set a bound which they [the waters] should not pass,
so that they might not again cover the earth.
Psalm 104:9

The experience of God as Creator does not lead to a meditation on endless stretches of infinity. It is, rather, a realization of boundaries (the framework and structure within which our habitation takes place) and obedience (the evidence that God's commanding word is obeyed).

PRAYER: Almighty God, Maker of heaven and earth, Creator of all the things I see and all the things I don't see: thank you for this carefully crafted world in which I can daily experience your love and your grace. All praise to you in Jesus Christ. *Amen.*

216.
"The Earth Is Satisfied"

Read Psalm 104:10–13

From thy lofty abode thou waterest the mountains;
the earth is satisfied with the fruit of thy work.
Psalm 104:13

The very environment in which we live is evidence of provision for our basic needs; fulfillments are built into the basic structure of creation. God the maker is also God the satisfier.

PRAYER: I turn my dissatisfactions over to you, O God. I know that every need I experience is a stimulus to come to you. I know that you have a way of dealing with each need so that I will live completed, not deprived; praising, not complaining. *Amen.*

217.
"Man Goes Forth to His Work"

Read Psalm 104:14–23

Man goes forth to his work
and to his labor until the evening.
Psalm 104:23

There is a detailed thoughtfulness evident throughout creation. As man goes about his daily work he realizes not only that it is richly furnished with all the resources he needs for his living, but that all other parts of creation are quite as well taken care of as he is. The Creator is not austere.

PRAYER: I walk in wonder through this world which you, O God, made and called good. You forgot nothing. You left nothing out. I will never, it seems, come to the end of discovering what is before my eyes and never run out of reasons for lifting up my discoveries in praise to your great name. *Amen.*

218.
"Living Things Both Small and Great"

Read Psalm 104:24–26

O LORD, how manifold are thy works!
In wisdom hast thou made them all;
the earth is full of thy creatures.
Yonder is the sea, great and wide,
which teems with things innumerable,
living things both small and great.
Psalm 104:24–25

The range of creation, from small to great, is staggering. There is an intricacy and extravagance in living forms that embraces rotifers and giraffes, dragonflies and whales. Clearly, there is exuberance and delight in the Creator.

PRAYER: "All things bright and beautiful, all creatures great and small, all things wise and wonderful; the Lord God made them all. . . . He gave us eyes to see them, and lips that we might tell how great is God Almighty, who has made all things well." *Amen.*
(Cecil Frances Alexander, "All Things Bright and Beautiful")

219.
"When Thou Sendest Forth Thy Spirit"
Read Psalm 104:27–30

When thou sendest forth thy Spirit, they are created;
and thou renewest the face of the ground.
Psalm 104:30

The pulsing creation in all its interrelated parts is as dependent upon the Creator Spirit as the human body is upon its respiratory system. The Spirit of God "moving over the face of the waters" in creation (Gen. 1:2) also supports and renews daily life.

PRAYER: Send your Spirit, Father. My inner life disintegrates without daily infusions of your Spirit. My energy for love dissipates without fresh visitations of your love. My faith atrophies without exercise in your grace. I receive, gratefully, what you give in Jesus Christ. *Amen.*

220.
"May My Meditation Be Pleasing"
Read Psalm 104:31–35

May my meditation be pleasing to him,
for I rejoice in the LORD.
Psalm 104:34

The Christian is in a position to realize the present, daily effects of creation—what it means to live in a world made and maintained by the Creator God. The last line of this psalm repeats the first and adds the one word, *Hallelujah* ("Praise the Lord"). The great praise word occurs only in the Psalms and for the first time here.

PRAYER: Great and eternal God: I immerse myself in your creation and gradually begin to comprehend the inventive attention you bring to each detail—and then realize that I am one of the details! Hallelujah! *Amen.*

221.
"Seek ... Remember"

Read Psalm 105:1–6

Seek the Lord and his strength,
    seek his presence continually!
Remember the wonderful works that he has done,
    his miracles, and the judgments he uttered.
Psalm 105:4–5

The linking of "seek the Lord" with "remember the wonderful works" connects worship with history, our recurrent needs with God's faithful acts. Our aspiring reach for God and God's descent to us in works of mercy and salvation parallel and synchronize in the gospel.

PRAYER: When I seek you, O God, I do it in a world full of your working. My asking is all done in the environment of your answers. Thank you for the needs which bring me back continuously to what only you can give, even in Jesus Christ. *Amen.*

222.
"Mindful of His Covenant"

Read Psalm 105:7–11

He is the Lord our God;
    his judgments are in all the earth.
He is mindful of his covenant for ever,
    of the word that he commanded, for a thousand generations.
Psalm 105:7–8

The word *covenant* releases to the memory numerous instances in which God has kept his agreement to love and lead his people, however indifferent or rebellious they have been. God's covenant is his commitment to us: he never forgets what he has decreed and never fails to keep what he has promised.

PRAYER: O God, I thank you for your unshakable decision to be my Savior and my Friend, a decision proven and ratified in Jesus Christ, by whose life I live. *Amen.*

223.
"Of Little Account"

Read Psalm 105:12–15

When they were few in number,
of little account, and sojourners in it,

· ·

he allowed no one to oppress them;
he rebuked kings on their account.

Psalm 105:12, 14

God's people can look back to a time when, though they were a mere handful of wandering refugees, they were absolutely safe in God's protection. We do not find our security by joining a strong and successful group, but by being servants to a strong and competent Savior. If we are "of little account" in the world's eyes, we are "in God's sight chosen and precious" (1 Pet. 2:4).

PRAYER: "Through each perplexing path of life our wandering footsteps guide; give us each day our daily bread, and raiment fit provide. O spread Thy covering wings around till all our wanderings cease, and at our Father's loved abode our souls arrive in peace." *Amen.*

(Phillip Doddridge, "O God of Bethel, by Whose Hand")

224.
"He Had Sent a Man Ahead"

Read Psalm 105:16–22

When he summoned a famine on the land,
and broke every staff of bread,
he had sent a man ahead of them,
Joseph, who was sold as a slave.

Psalm 105:16–17

The story of Joseph is continuously useful to the person of faith. It shows that no matter how calamitously world events seem to fall in upon us, God has anticipated our troubles and prepared a way for our salvation. God has been there ahead of us. In difficult times the Christian is surprised, not by disaster, but by providence.

PRAYER: Dear Father, thank you for looking after me by sending Jesus ahead of me through temptation and suffering, so that with confidence I can walk through "the valley of the shadow" and know that nothing will separate me from the love you have for me. In Jesus' name. *Amen.*

(Ps. 23:4)

225.
"Stronger Than Their Foes"

Read Psalm 105:23–25

And the LORD made his people very fruitful,
and made them stronger than their foes.
Psalm 105:24

The Egyptians looked on the ancient Israelites as slaves and demeaned them; the Israelites understood themselves as servants of God and experienced deliverance. The Romans looked on the early Christians as criminals and persecuted them; the Christians confessed themselves as sinners and found freedom in Christ. Similar reversals of weakness and strength occur in every life of faith.

PRAYER: O God, when I feel incapable of good and worthless for love, I will remember your words to St. Paul; "My grace is sufficient for you, for my power is made perfect in weakness," and I will take heart, even in Jesus Christ in whose name I pray. *Amen.*

(2 Cor. 12:9)

226.
"Miracles in the Land of Ham"

Read Psalm 105:26–36

He sent Moses his servant,
and Aaron whom he had chosen.
They wrought his signs among them,
and miracles in the land of Ham.
Psalm 105:26–27

The Egyptian plagues have always seemed especially apt evidence of the power of God. In each instance the plague consisted of something which in itself was common, harmless, weak or unimpressive. Solely by the work of God it was transformed into a powerful instrument of his will.

PRAYER: Dear God, I know that you can use anything to bring about your purposes, even things that I treat as unimportant, even areas of life that seem to me to be remote from the divine mercy. Grant that I may be alert to your will in every thing and in every place. *Amen.*

227.
"None...Stumbled"

Read Psalm 105:37–41

Then he led forth Israel with silver and gold,
and there was none among his tribes who stumbled.
Psalm 105:37

In the world of nature, especially in times of stress, the strong survive and the weak are discarded. In the world of grace there is none of that; the weak are provided for as well as the strong. Escape from Egypt is not a horror story of desperate scrambling, but a salvation story of gracious providence in which God gathers all his people to new life.

PRAYER: "Lead, kindly Light, amid th' encircling gloom, lead Thou me on; the night is dark, and I am far from home; lead Thou me on: keep Thou my feet; I do not ask to see the distant scene—one step enough for me." *Amen.*

(John Henry Newman, "Lead, Kindly Light")

228.
"He Led Forth His People With Joy"

Read Psalm 105:43–45

So he led forth his people with joy,
his chosen ones with singing.
Psalm 105:43

Faith examines history for evidence of God's acts—protecting, leading, sustaining, promising, fulfilling. Thirty-four times in this psalm active verbs have God as their subject. Our interest in history is not so much in *what happened* as in *who made it happen.*

PRAYER: Dear Father, while others examine the past for evidence of human accomplishments, gathering material to rationalize pride, give me the ability to see it as a record of your covenant faithfulness, the gracious acts by which all men may experience your love and salvation. *Amen.*

229.
"Remember Me, O Lord"

Read Psalm 106:1–5

Remember me, O Lord, when thou showest favor to thy people;
help me when thou deliverest them;
Psalm 106:4

In light of the fact that the body of this psalm (vv. 6–39) will consist of a lamentation for and confession of sin, the opening praise is significant. It is because the Lord "is good" and "his steadfast love endures forever" that sin can be confessed with the expectation ("remember me") of restoration.

PRAYER: As I look at the past I see a mass of human failings; keep me, O God, from adding yet another sin by using what I see to document accusations against others. Rather, I will confess my contribution to the failures and look to you for forgiveness, in Jesus Christ. *Amen.*

230.
"We and Our Fathers Have Sinned"

Read Psalm 106:6–12

Both we and our fathers have sinned;
we have committed iniquity,
we have done wickedly.
Psalm 106:6

In the exodus God worked his mightiest act of salvation. But Israel's part in it was ignominious; at the crisis she was rebellious, obdurate and without either intelligence or faith. The people offered God nothing but their sin; God responded with an invincible grace.

PRAYER: Father, the more I realize the depth and deviousness of my sin, the more I realize the persistence and power of your grace. How I thank you for coming to me in salvation in Jesus Christ! *Amen.*

231.
"Soon Forgot His Works"

Read Psalm 106:13–18

But they soon forgot his works;
they did not wait for his counsel.
Psalm 106:13

Forgetfulness (v. 13) and insurrection (v. 16) are often found paired. When we forget God's ways of providing for us, we impatiently seek to set up our own self-government. And our rebellious attempts to lead ourselves can be carried out only in an atmosphere devoid of the memory of grace.

PRAYER: Merciful Lord, grant that my remembrance of your ways will lead me to a more trusting obedience, and grant that my obedience may improve my memory, so that I may not forget anything you have done for me or quarrel with any of your commands. *Amen.*

232.
"They Exchanged the Glory of God"

Read Psalm 106:19–27

They exchanged the glory of God
for the image of an ox that eats grass.
Psalm 106:20

Neither going to church nor staying home is proof against sin. The psalmist collects instances that document sin's perverseness, the seemingly unending ways in which sin may erupt in our worship ("worshiped a molten image") and in our homes ("murmured in their tents").

PRAYER: "Cure Thy children's warring madness, bend our pride to Thy control; shame our wanton, selfish gladness, rich in things and poor in soul. Grant us wisdom, grant us courage, lest we miss Thy Kingdom's goal." *Amen.*

(Harry Emerson Fosdick, "God of Grace and God of Glory")

233.
"The Baal of Peor"

Read Psalm 106:28–31

> Then they attached themselves to the Baal of Peor,
> and ate sacrifices offered to the dead.
> *Psalm 106:28*

The sin at Baal Peor (see Num. 25), a particularly vile form of orgy, was a religious act which comprised worship and sacrifice, a combination of the faith of the fathers and the cult of Canaan. Mature faith, however, is not a result of assimilating every religion we touch, but of choosing God in every aspect of our existence.

PRAYER: O God, you have given me the ability to choose; now strengthen my will to choose your lordship. Give me a discriminating mind so that I can discern your ways among all the tempting alternatives, in the name of Jesus Christ. *Amen.*

234.
"The Waters of Meribah"

Read Psalm 106:32–33

> They angered him at the waters of Meribah,
> and it went ill with Moses on their account;
> for they made his spirit bitter,
> and he spoke words that were rash.
> *Psalm 106:32–33*

The story of faith is studded with place names that recall God's grace; Bethel, Sinai, Carmel, Olivet. But there are as many others that are memories of man's sin—Meribah is one of those. The geography of salvation shows desirable places to go and troublesome routes to avoid.

PRAYER: I forget, Lord, how dangerously my discontent can affect another's trust. I want to be especially considerate of those who are leaders and companions in the way of faith, supporting them with appreciation and intercession, not toppling them with criticism and grumbling. *Amen.*

235.
"The Land Was Polluted"

Read Psalm 106:34–39

They poured out innocent blood,
  the blood of their sons and daughters,
whom they sacrificed to the idols of Canaan;
  and the land was polluted with blood.
Psalm 106:38

The years of conquest were inglorious. What might have been a triumphant claiming of promises became a long series of defections and compromises; instead of sharing faith in a holy God, Israel adopted the savage rites of child sacrifice. The land which, in promise, flowed "with milk and honey," in disobedience flowed with the blood of innocent children.

PRAYER: "Save us from weak resignation to the evils we deplore; let the search for Thy salvation be our glory evermore. Grant us wisdom, grant us courage, serving Thee whom we adore." *Amen.*
(Harry Emerson Fosdick, "God of Grace and God of Glory")

236.
"Nevertheless"

Read Psalm 106:40–46

Then the anger of the LORD was kindled against his people....
....
Nevertheless he regarded their distress,
  when he heard their cry.
Psalm 106:40, 44

Man connects cause and effect with a *therefore;* God connects them with a *nevertheless.* The logical consequence of sin is damnation; the gospel consequence is salvation. *Nevertheless* is one of the most important words in Scripture, for it miraculously joins man's sin with God's salvation.

PRAYER: What a happy discovery, O God, to find that each act of confession is not an occasion for condemnation but an experience of your forgiveness: "Make mercy in all of us, out of us all/Mastery, but be adored, but be adored King." *Amen.*
(Gerard Manley Hopkins, "The Wreck of the Deutschland")

237.
"Gather Us"

Read Psalm 106:47–48

Save us, O Lord our God,
 and gather us from among the nations,
 that we may give thanks to thy holy name
 and glory in thy praise.

Psalm 106:47

The proper response for one who lives in a culture permeated with sin is not to wash his hands of it (Pilate's futile gesture), nor to separate himself from it with rites of imagined purification; it is to engage in prayers of intercession for God's mercy and to give praise for his salvation.

PRAYER: Lord Jesus Christ, you took all sin upon yourself that you might free me from its death. "There is therefore now no condemnation!" I praise you for your bold mercy. *Amen.*

(Rom. 8:1)

238.
"Say So"

Read Psalm 107:1–3

Let the redeemed of the Lord say so,
 whom he has redeemed from trouble.

Psalm 107:2

The redeemed are summoned from the four quarters of the compass to give vigorous witness to God's goodness and God's love. As the roll is called, representative figures are announced to step forth and give a personal report on the ways in which redemption is experienced: "Let the redeemed of the Lord say so!"

PRAYER: I give thanks to you, O Lord. I have experienced your goodness and know it is working in me; I have experienced your love and know that it is changing me. Thank you, in the name of Jesus Christ, my Redeemer. *Amen.*

239.
"The Hungry He Fills with Good Things"

Read Psalm 107:4–9

> For he satisfies him who is thirsty,
> and the hungry he fills with good things.
> *Psalm 107:9*

Hunger and thirst are daily reminders that we have needs. We cannot exist without help. We are not self-contained. But God has not only created needs in us, he has provided fulfillments for us. Every meal eaten, every cup of water drunk, is a sign of the satisfactions God provides in his creative providence and redemptive mercy.

PRAYER: "O could I speak the matchless worth, O could I sound the glories forth which in my Saviour shine! I'd sing His glorious righteousness, and magnify the wondrous grace which made salvation mine." *Amen.*

(Samuel Medley, "O Could I Speak the Matchless Worth")

240.
"He Shatters the Doors of Bronze"

Read Psalm 107:10–16

> For he shatters the doors of bronze,
> and cuts in two the bars of iron.
> *Psalm 107:16*

There are life situations that appear to be absolutely without hope. Sometimes our own actions put us in such dungeons; sometimes the actions of others are responsible. But however we get there, there is no getting out. And then God rescues us: from Egypt, from Babylon, from Calvary, from sin, from death.

PRAYER: Shatter the doors of bronze that shut me up in guilt, O God; cut the bars of iron that lock me into doubt. Release me into the free land of the forgiven; lead me into the open spaces of faith for Jesus' sake. *Amen.*

241.
"And Healed Them"

Read Psalm 107:17–22

> Some were sick through their sinful ways,
> and because of their iniquities suffered affliction;
> . . . .
> he sent forth his word, and healed them,
> and delivered them from destruction.
>
> *Psalm 107:17, 20*

Sin is bad for health. Many illnesses (though not all) are a consequence of moral disorder. Salvation, however, brings wholeness. When we are responsive to God's delivering, healing word in Christ, we find not only our spirits renewed but our bodies regenerated by their Creator.

PRAYER: I submit myself, God, to your care and providence. I put myself, body and spirit, in your care: correct, guide, heal, restore. Be to me the Great Physician, even in Jesus Christ. *Amen.*

242.
"At Their Wits' End"

Read Psalm 107:23–32

> They reeled and staggered like drunken men,
> and were at their wits' end.
>
> *Psalm 107:27*

In the world of business, men see the successful application of their intelligence to the complexities of trade and commerce and acquire a sense of control. But there are powers and forces over which cunning has no influence. Life has storms from which mere ingenuity cannot save us.

PRAYER: Just when I get my life arranged so that everything is under control, something happens to upset it. I need to learn, Lord, that life is not a business that I arrange and control, but a pilgrimage in which you give protection and provide guidance. Help me to learn that through Jesus Christ, my Lord. *Amen.*

243.
"A Desert into Pools of Water"

Read Psalm 107:33–38

He turns a desert into pools of water,
a parched land into springs of water.
Psalms 107:35

Rivers can dry up and deserts can blossom. The world as we find
it is neither a guarantee of happiness nor a condemnation to despair.
Not the ground we put our feet on but the God we put our trust in
provides a sure, unchanging base on which to live.

PRAYER: Great God, I will neither divinize this earth you have
given nor abhor it; not turn the river into a god; not turn the desert
into a demon. I will enjoy your largesse in the pleasant places and
obey your will in the difficult straits, as you direct and enable me in
Jesus Christ. *Amen.*

244.
"Whoever Is Wise"

Read Psalm 107:39–43

Whoever is wise, let him give heed to these things;
let men consider the steadfast love of the LORD.
Psalm 107:43

The psalm spotlights five areas in which men experience God's
saving power and, in each instance, calls for appropriate praise. Wise
men are conversant with the ways in which God works and are practiced in making glad response.

PRAYER: Almighty God, you satisfy and you deliver; you heal and
you rescue; you judge and you bless. I will give heed to all that you
do; I will pay attention to the ways you show love; I will be glad in
Jesus Christ. *Amen.*

245.
"I Will Awake the Dawn!"

Read Psalm 108:1-6

My heart is steadfast, O God, my heart is steadfast!
I will sing and make melody!
. . . .
I will awake the dawn!

Psalm 108:1-2

Dawn, the signal for waking up and going about our work, is herself awakened by the praising man. Eager to plunge into a daily round where "grace is everywhere" (George Bernanos, *Diary of a Country Priest*, p. 232), he rouses the world around him to a life of praise.

PRAYER: "When morning gilds the skies, my heart awaking cries, may Jesus Christ be praised: alike at work and prayer to Jesus I repair; may Jesus Christ be praised! The night becomes as day when from the heart we say, may Jesus Christ be praised: the powers of darkness fear when this sweet chant they hear, may Jesus Christ be praised!" *Amen.*

("When Morning Gilds the Skies," German, trans. by Edward Caswell)

246.
"Moab Is My Washbasin"

Read Psalm 108:7-9

God has promised in his sanctuary:
. . . .
"Moab is my washbasin;
   upon Edom I cast my shoe;
   over Phillistia I shout in triumph."

Psalm 108:7, 9

Everyday names are used to dramatize redemption: portions of the promised land (Shechem, Succoth, Gilead, Manasseh, Ephraim, Judah) become instruments for God's rule, while traditionally hostile nations (Moab, Edom, Philistia) are subordinated to God's victory. The eternal story of salvation is localized in the familiar vocabulary of geography.

PRAYER: O God, I want to acquire a lively sense of your active rule in the towns and nations around me—to experience your promises and be confident of your victory, through Jesus Christ, my Lord and Savior. *Amen.*

247.
"With God We Shall Do Valiantly"

Read Psalm 108:10–13

With God we shall do valiantly;
it is he who will tread down our foes.
Psalm 108:13

Edom, with its rocky fortress capital of Petra, had a reputation for being absolutely impregnable. In the life of faith it has become a symbol for the forces of sin—forces before which man is powerless but which are conquered routinely by God in Christ.

PRAYER: I thank you, O God, for delivering me from a way of life bound by impossibilities into one that burgeons with opportunities. I will no longer live timidly and cautiously, inhibited by the enemy, but confidently and valiantly, believing in a victorious Jesus Christ. *Amen.*

248.
"Be Not Silent"

Read Psalm 109:1–5

Be not silent, O God of my praise!
For wicked and deceitful mouths are opened against me,
speaking against me with lying tongues.
Psalm 109:1–2

Can man's noisy condemnations ever drown out the voice of God? Can the rude accusations of men ever silence God's acceptance? The testimony of men who pray is that they cannot. God speaks—in Scripture, in sacrament, in the "still small voice" (1 Kings 19:12). He speaks; he is not silent.

PRAYER: Father, sometimes I think that you have stopped speaking, and then I discover that it is I who have stopped listening. Restore the hearing that has grown dull in disobedience, and then repeat the words I need to hear in faith. *Amen.*

249.
"He Did Not Like Blessing"

Read Psalm 109:6–19

He loved to curse; let curses come on him!
He did not like blessing; may it be far from him!
Psalm 109:17

If we choose to curse, cursing is the environment we finally inhabit, inescapably. If we oppress, oppression is the context in which we exist, unavoidably. Our words and our acts create conditions in which we ourselves must live. Unrepentant and unforgiven, we live with the curses and pitiless actions which we set loose in the world.

PRAYER: God, teach me the pure speech of praise and the exalted speech of blessing. Help me to avoid blasphemous and complaining words as readily as I resist diseased and contaminated objects. May my "speech always be gracious, seasoned with salt," so that I may bring glory to your name. *Amen.*

(Col. 4:6)

250.
"But Do Thou Bless"

Read Psalm 109:20–29

Let them curse, but do thou bless!
Let my assailants be put to shame; may thy servant be glad!
Psalm 109:28

Our lives are not determined by popular vote. "Hid with Christ in God" (Col. 3:3), we are beyond the fashions and opinions of men. If we are an "object of scorn" to many, we are recipients of "steadfast love" through Jesus Christ (vv. 25, 26). The blessing of God is far more determinitive for our lives than the curses of men.

PRAYER: Father, like Jacob at Peniel, I wrestle and wait. Only your blessing can give me what I need; only your blessing can make me whole. O God "from whom all blessings flow," bless me. In Jesus' name. *Amen.*

"At the Right Hand of the Needy"

Read Psalm 109:30–31

> With my mouth I will give great thanks to the LORD;
> I will praise him in the midst of the throng.
> For he stands at the right hand of the needy,
> to save him from those who condemn him to death.
> *Psalm 109:30–31*

Ours is not a storybook god, a heroic figure out of a mythical past. Nor is he a philosophical god, a divine idea available to clever minds for answering questions about life. God is he whom we need at our right hand to save us from condemnation.

PRAYER: "God be in my head, and in my understanding; God be in mine eyes, and in my looking; God be in my mouth, and in my speaking; God be in my heart, and in my thinking; God be at mine end, and at my departing." *Amen.*

(Sarum Primer)

252.
"Sit at My Right Hand"

Read Psalm 110

> The LORD says to my lord:
> "Sit at my right hand,
> till I make your enemies
> your footstool."
> *Psalm 110:1*

To the first-century Christian, every line in this psalm was fulfilled in Jesus, God's Christ. As a result, no psalm was more frequently quoted. In the very history in which the world supposed that it saw the defeat of God, the Christian faith realized God's majestic rule in resurrection.

PRAYER: High and lifted up, O Lord, you center my aspirations, preside over my growth and rule my will. You are Lord to me in majesty and mercy. All praise to your great name. *Amen.*

253.
"Your People Will Offer Themselves"

Read Psalm 110:1–4

Your people will offer themselves freely
on the day you lead your host
upon the holy mountains.
Psalm 110:3

Messiah reunites in his person ancient orders of kingship and priesthood. The king represented power to rule, shape and guide life. The priest represented power to renew, forgive and invigorate life. The offices are personalized and integrated in Messiah so attractively that response is spontaneous.

PRAYER: Lord Jesus Christ: rule me and renew me. Establish the purposes of creation in my life; release the energies of the covenant in the responses of my spirit. I freely offer myself to what you are and what you do. *Amen.*

254.
"He Will Drink from the Brook"

Read Psalm 110:5–7

He will drink from the brook by the way;
therefore he will lift up his head.
Psalm 110:7

After completing the work of redemption and judgment, leading his people to victory and leaving his enemies in disarray, Messiah drinks from the brook—a moment of renewal: "There is a river whose streams make glad the city of God" (Ps. 46:4).

PRAYER: "Rise, God, judge Thou the earth in might, this wicked earth redress; for Thou art He who shall by right the nations all possess. For great Thou art, and wonders great by Thy strong hand are done; Thou in Thy everlasting seat remainest God alone." *Amen.*

(John Milton, "Rise, God, Judge Thou the Earth in Might")

137

255.
"His Praise Endures Forever!"

Ps 111:5 -- I'm ever on G's mind bec I'm a cov person.
So get in your cov. w/ G.

Read Psalm 111

The fear of the LORD is the beginning of wisdom;
a good understanding have all those who practice it.
His praise endures for ever!
Psalm 111:10

Do we think praise is the natural exuberance of the contented person? It is not—it is the thoughtful response of the redeemed. It springs, not from man's good feelings, but from God's good acts. We praise God, not when we feel good, but when we realize that God is good.

PRAYER: I will remember and observe your goodness through the hours of this day, O God, keeping in mind what you have done faithfully through centuries of redemption and staying alert to what you presently are doing in the lives of companions in faith. And I will use all I remember and observe to lift praises to you. *Amen.*

256.
"His Heart is Firm"

Read Psalm 112

Praise the LORD.
Blessed is the man who fears the LORD,
who greatly delights in his commandments!
· ·
He is not afraid of evil tidings;
his heart is firm, trusting in the LORD.
Psalm 112:1, 7

Anyone whose sense of well-being depends upon stock-market quotations, weather forecasts, or the statistics of a public opinion pollster will be constantly on edge, "afraid of evil tidings." The person who listens in faith to God's word and responds in praise, however, has foundations of eternity built into the structures of his soul and thereby acquires a firm heart.

PRAYER: God Almighty: listening to your words and responding to your commands, I build on the rock that is Christ. Let no wind or storm shake my commitment or compromise the praise that I offer up to you in Jesus' name. *Amen.*

257.
"He Raises the Poor"

Who is like the LORD our God ... ?
....
He raises the poor from the dust,
and lifts the needy from the ash heap,
to make them sit with princes,
with the princes of his people.
Psalm 113:1, 7–8

God's people know that he enters into whatever despair in which we feel condemned and then lifts us into his purposes in Jesus Christ. The story of every soul in Christ has an upward thrust and a joyous goal.

PRAYER: I search my own heart, O God, and find cause only for humiliation and despair. I look around at the world and see only degradation and defeat. And then I lift my eyes to you and see redemption and love. Praise the Lord! *Amen.*

258.
"The Mountains Skipped like Rams"

When Israel went forth from Egypt,
the house of Jacob from a people of strange language,
....
The mountains skipped like rams,
the hills like lambs.
Psalm 114:1, 4

The stolid mountains dance a jig; the placid sea runs for cover; the dour rock springs a fountain. The whole world, in ecstasy, responds to God's love expressed in salvation.

PRAYER: God, I stumble upon wonder after wonder—and every wonder true. I hardly comprehend the awesome majesty of your acts; I barely realize the immense mercy of your will. I worship and adore you, through Jesus Christ. *Amen.*

259.
"Idols"

Read Psalm 115:1–8

Their idols are silver and gold,
the work of men's hands.
Psalm 115:4

"Surely, just as waters boil up from a vast, full spring, so does an immense crowd of gods flow forth from the human mind, while each one, in wandering about with too much license, wrongly invents this or that about God himself. . . . man's nature, so to speak, is a perpetual factory of idols" (John Calvin, *Institutes of the Christian Religion,* 1: 65, 108).

PRAYER: Father Almighty, you revealed yourself to me in Jesus Christ, "full of grace and truth." Cure me of idol-making, from fashioning gods out of my desire and imagination, so that I can be free to worship you—Father, Son, and Holy Spirit. *Amen.*

(John 1:14)

260.
"Their Help and Their Shield"

Read Psalm 115:9–18

O Israel, trust in the LORD!
He is their help and their shield.
Psalm 115:9

We do not make God; he makes us. We do not take care of him; he takes care of us. We do not invent new attributes and duties for him; he creatively leads us into new styles of obedience and experiences of blessings. This realization evokes responses of trust and praise.

PRAYER: I give glory to your name, O God: I will say words that are obedient to your commands and engage in acts that express your love. I will put the workings of my mind and the movements of my body to your service, in trust and praise. *Amen.*

261.
"He Has Heard My Voice"

Read Psalm 116:1–4

I love the LORD, because he has heard
my voice and my supplications.
Psalm 116:1

It is marvelous that God speaks to us—life-giving, world-creating words. This marvel is matched by another—that he listens to us. His listening gives all our words significance and makes all our prayers personal.

PRAYER: I have times of desperation, O God, when I suppose that you neither speak nor listen. When that happens bring me back to this psalm and to Jesus Christ, who also felt despair and now lives to make intercession for me. *Amen.*

262.
"Land of the Living"

Read Psalm 116:5–11

For thou hast delivered my soul from death,
my eyes from tears,
my feet from stumbling;
I walk before the LORD
in the land of the living.
Psalm 116:8–9

This man had exhausted his personal resources—he could not help himself ("I am greatly afflicted"). He had, additionally, found that friends were either unable or unwilling to help him ("men are all a vain hope"). The only remaining recourse was God. And God, gracious and righteous and merciful, saved him.

PRAYER: "Jesus, my All in all Thou art: my rest in toil, my ease in pain, the healing of my broken heart, in war my peace, in loss my gain, my smile beneath the tyrant's frown, in shame my glory and my crown." *Amen.*

(Charles Wesley, "Thou Hidden Source of Calm Repose")

263.
"What Shall I Render to the Lord?"

Read Psalm 116:12–19

What shall I render to the LORD
for all his bounty to me?
Psalm 116:12

The completeness of salvation accomplished in Jesus Christ means that there is no "work" left for us to do. But we are not thereby consigned to passivity. As active participants in the world of grace we lift the cup of salvation, pay vows and offer the sacrifice of thanksgiving—acts of celebration, obedience, and praise.

PRAYER: God, though I had no part in causing salvation I can at least be part of its celebration, heartily and often, in the name of Jesus Christ. Fuse obedience and praise into a perfect unity of response in me. *Amen.*

264.
"Great is His Steadfast Love"

Read Psalm 117

For great is his steadfast love toward us;
and the faithfulness of the LORD endures for ever.
Praise the LORD!
Psalm 117:2

Here is a perfect concentration of meditation and response: all that God is to us (steadfast love . . . faithfulness) evokes all that we can be to him (praise the Lord . . . extol him.).

PRAYER: "Holy, holy, holy, is the Lord God Almighty, who was and is and is to come! . . . Worthy art thou, our Lord and God, to receive glory and honor and power, for thou didst create all things, and by thy will they existed and were created." *Amen.*

(Rev. 4:8, 11)

265.
"Let Israel Say"

Read Psalm 118:1–4

Let Israel say,
"His steadfast love endures for ever."
Psalm 118:2

When every incident in the experience of the people under God was discovered to be an exposition of God's steadfast love, then every gathering of those people came to be an expression of gratitude. "In this is love, not that we loved God but that he loved us and sent his Son to be the expiation for our sins" (1 John 4:10).

PRAYER: "The King of love my Shepherd is, whose goodness faileth never; I nothing lack if I am His and He is mine forever. . . . And so through all the length of days Thy goodness faileth never: Good Shepherd, may I sing Thy praise within Thy house forever." *Amen.*
(Henry W. Baker, "The King of Love My Shepherd Is")

266.
"The Lord Helped Me"

Read Psalm 118:5–14

I was pushed hard, so that I was falling,
but the LORD helped me.
Psalm 118:13

Prayer does not produce "weak resignation to the evils we deplore" (Fosdick) but strenuous battle against the powers of destruction. God does not lead us to bow our heads quietly in submission; he invigorates us to moral battle. "I can do all things in him who strengthens me" (Phil. 4:13).

PRAYER: Grant, O God, that by your Spirit I may find motive and means to speak and act in your name. I need courage to face all the skirmishes of daily living and confidence in your promises given in Jesus Christ, in whose name I pray. *Amen.*

267.
"Glad Songs of Victory"

Read Psalm 118:15–18

Hark, glad songs of victory
in the tents of the righteous:
"The right hand of the LORD does valiantly... !"
Psalm 118:15

The community of the people of God reverberates with victorious praise. The gospel is life-affirming and death-defeating. "Thanks be to God for his inexpressible gift!" (2 Cor. 9:15).

PRAYER: Dear God, every sin that I thought was a barrier between you and me has been, by your grace, made into a bridge. You have used the very things that separate us as ways to approach me with new life. Thank you. *Amen.*

268.
"Gates of Righteousness"

Read Psalm 118:19–20

Open to me the gates of righteousness,
that I may enter through them
and give thanks to the LORD.
Psalm 118:19

Biblical faith is characterized by a vocabulary of access and invitation—well-marked approaches to follow and wonderfully courteous invitations to accept. Faith is access to God, and discipleship is entrance into his joy.

PRAYER: I don't want my life, Lord, to be a meandering stream, its course altered by every stone and diverted by each depression, following the path of least resistance. I want it to be a direct, undiverted flow through the wide, inviting gates that lead to your will in Jesus Christ. *Amen.*

269.
"The Head of the Corner"

Read Psalm 118:21–25

The stone which the builders rejected
has become the head of the corner.
Psalm 118:22

God provides the gift of life, but our death-conditioned minds do not recognize it. It is so foreign to all that we are used to that we discard it, unrecognized. But God does not accept our rejection. He comes again and uses what we have rejected to build our lives in salvation and to hold us together in eternity.

PRAYER: God, my imagination is faithless and my faith is unimaginative. How often I fail to see and use what is right before me! How often I impatiently discard the very thing you have patiently provided to help me in my need! Overcome all my impatient rejections with your patient acceptance of me in Jesus Christ. *Amen.*

270.
"Festal Procession"

Read Psalm 118:26–27

The LORD is God,
and he has given us light.
Bind the festal procession with branches,
up to the horns of the altar!
Psalm 118:27

All the elements in the psalm—the surprises of love, the gifts of victory, the discoveries of salvation—are assembled and then marched in a parade of celebration. Worship gathers all the experiences of grace and binds them together in festal response.

PRAYER: God, make every gathering with friends in Christ a time of blessing. Create a readiness to receive from you and a faithfulness to respond to you, so that all you give in love and all we bring in praise may be fire on your altar. *Amen.*

271.
"Thou Art My God"

Read Psalm 118:28–29

Thou art my God, and I will give thanks to thee;
thou art my God, I will extol thee.
Psalm 118:28

The more we know of God the more we have cause to praise him. As our knowledge increases our thanksgiving develops. Every discovery of goodness and love is provocation to praise.

PRAYER: Because I know your goodness, O God, I can recognize goodness in the world around me. Thank you. Because I experience your steadfast love I can give and receive love among the people around me. Thank you. Receive all my thanksgivings in and through Jesus Christ. *Amen.*

272.
"Blessed Are Those..."

Read Psalm 119:1

Blessed are those whose way is blameless,
who walk in the law of the LORD!
Psalm 119:1

What a remarkable attitude to God's law! In this—the longest and, in many ways, the most remarkable of psalms—there is an astonishing inventiveness for expressing delight in God's law. There seems to be no bottom to its exuberance and no limit to its enjoyment. God's revelation consists not of hard rules to be kept, nor of restrictive limitations to be endured, but of ways to walk in happiness and praise.

PRAYER: Almighty God, you have given me such great words of guidance and grace; I accept them as gifts to be embraced in joy. Thank you for a law which can be enjoyed and celebrated, in the name of Jesus Christ. *Amen.*

273.
"Whole Heart"

Read Psalm 119:2–8

Blessed are those who keep his testimonies,
who seek him with their whole heart.
Psalm 119:2

The law of God is not regulations to keep us religious, and it is not rules to keep us moral. It is "the whole counsel of God" which creates, preserves and redeems. The only adequate response from man is the "whole heart"—a total revelation requires a total response.

PRAYER: Father, you have anticipated everything that I need and have given me wise words of command, instruction and comfort to surround every circumstance. As I listen and believe, accomplish your will in me for Jesus' sake. *Amen.*

274.
"Thy Word in My Heart"

Read Psalm 119:9–16

I have laid up thy word in my heart,
that I might not sin against thee.
Psalm 119:11

The heart well-stocked with God's word is like a well-armed arsenal. Confident in the strength of its weaponry, it is fearless in the face of attacks from without or insurrection from within.

PRAYER: "Thy word is like an armory, where soldiers may repair, and find for life's long battle day all needful weapons there. O may I find my armor there: Thy Word my trusty sword, I'll learn to fight with every foe the battle of the Lord." *Amen.*

(Edwin Hodder, "Thy Word Is Like a Garden, Lord")

275.
"Open My Eyes"

Read Psalm 119:17–24

> Open my eyes, that I may behold
> wondrous things out of thy law.
> *Psalm 119:18*

When we find ourselves deficient in wisdom, it is not because the Word of God has pages missing, but because we have not seen all there is on the pages we already have. It is not another book we need, but better attention to the book we have; it is not more knowledge we require, but better vision to see what has already been revealed in Jesus Christ.

PRAYER: Father, as I read your counsels and commandments in Scripture, grant that I may not be drowsy or inattentive in my reading, but really see what is there with open, observant eyes, in Jesus' name. *Amen.*

276.
"I Cleave to Thy Testimonies"

Read Psalm 119:25–31

> My soul cleaves to the dust;
> revive me according to thy word!
> ....
> I cleave to thy testimonies, O LORD;
> let me not be put to shame!
> *Psalm 119:25, 31*

The man in despair ("My soul cleaves to the dust" v. 25) embraces God's word as a means of salvation ("I cleave to thy testimonies" v. 31) and is not disappointed. God gives hope to the downhearted and strength to the weak. His word is truth and tonic.

PRAYER: O God, forgive me for looking in all the wrong places for refreshment and renewal—I waste so much time trying out the promises of men. I return to your promises and find what I need: forgiveness and counsel and command, even in Jesus Christ. *Amen.*

277.
"I Will Run . . ."

Read Psalm 119:32

I will run in the way of thy commandments
when thou enlargest my understanding!
Psalm 119:32

God's commandments are not a tortured path to crawl along, nor a narrow trail to cling to, but a wide smooth path to run upon: "In the sun born over and over,/I ran my heedless ways" ("Fern Hill," Dylan Thomas).

PRAYER: How glorious, O God, to find that your commands do not oppress or restrict or cramp but set me free in a life of lightness and openness in Christ, in whose name I give thanks. *Amen.*

278.
"Teach Me, O Lord"

Read Psalm 119:33–40

Teach me, O LORD, the way of thy statutes;
and I will keep it to the end.
Psalm 119:33

Man's thirst for knowledge and hunger for wisdom are satisfied, finally, not in the schools or universities but in God. God teaches us our origins in his love and our destiny in his redemption. What else does a man need to know?

PRAYER: "Savior, teach me, day by day, love's sweet lesson, to obey; sweeter lesson cannot be, loving Him who first loved me. . . . Teach me thus Thy steps to trace, strong to follow in Thy grace, learning how to love from Thee, loving Him who first loved me." *Amen.*

(Jane Leeson, "Savior, Teach Me Day by Day")

279.
"Thy Commandments, Which I Love"

Read Psalm 119:41–48

> ... I find my delight in thy commandments,
> which I love.
>
> *Psalm 119:47*

Jesus summarized all the commandments of God by telling us to love God and to love our neighbor. This psalmist goes a step further and loves the commandments that tell him to love!

PRAYER: O God, your love creates me, redeems me and commands me. May all my responses to you be shaped in love, for the sake of Jesus Christ who first loved me. *Amen.*

280.
"Thy Promise Gives Me Life"

Read Psalm 119:49–53

> This is my comfort in my affliction
> that thy promise gives me life.
>
> *Psalm 119:50*

There is a difference between wishing and hoping: a wish is what men think will give them happiness; a hope is what men believe God will do to fulfill their lives. Wishes are based on human fantasies; hopes are based on God's promises.

PRAYER: Almighty God, I listen to your promises. Teach me to live in hope. I want you to perfect your love and complete your redemption in me. Thank you, O Lord of hope. *Amen.*

281.
"Thy Statutes ... My Songs"

Read Psalm 119:54–56

Thy statutes have been my songs
in the house of my pilgrimage.
Psalm 119:54

The psalmist made a songbook out of the commandments. And what happy tunes he must have set them to! And how many must have been glad to join him in his singing! Have God's commands ever been enjoyed as much as these?

PRAYER: Praise your great name, O God! You have given me such joy in obedience, such happiness in righteousness. Your words delight my heart while songs spring up unbidden as I walk your paths. *Amen.*

282.
"My Feet to Thy Testimonies"

Read Psalm 119:57–64

When I think of thy ways,
I turn my feet to thy testimonies.
Psalm 119:59

When the Christian thinks of God's promises and remembers God's ways, his first impulse is to act them out. Feet, not ears and tongues, are the organs of obedience. Dwight L. Moody used to say that every Bible should be bound in shoe leather.

PRAYER: Father, I would not stand around today in idleness talking about your will, nor sit indolently reading about your will. You have very graciously "shod" my "feet with the equipment of the gospel of peace"—I am well able now, by your grace, to walk in your will. In Jesus' name. *Amen.*

(Eph. 6:15)

283.
"Afflicted"

Read Psalm 119:65–72

Before I was afflicted I went astray;
but now I keep thy word.
Psalm 119:67

The people of God are grateful for afflictions which call them from wayward paths and bring them into more intimate dependence on his will. The ancient Greeks had a saying which reinforces the psalmist's experience: "Suffered things are learned things."

PRAYER: If suffering comes my way, O God, may I receive it as a means of being drawn closer to you, of learning your love, of discovering your mercy, of trusting your will, even as so many of your children have learned your ways through the school of affliction. *Amen.*

284.
"Let Thy Mercy Come"

Read Psalm 119:73–80

Let thy mercy come to me, that I may live;
for thy law is my delight.
Psalm 119:77

Anyone who thinks of the law of God as a ponderous legal document, passionless and abstract, has learned his definition in the wrong school. Law is not an abstraction of God's essence into books but the personalization of his will among men. The characteristic words associated with it are *hope, steadfast love, mercy.*

PRAYER: O God, may I never divorce my information about you from my experience with you; may I never separate what men tell me you are from what I believe you have become for me, even in Jesus Christ, in whose name I praise and serve you. *Amen.*

285.
"Like a Wineskin in the Smoke"

Read Psalm 119:81–88

> For I have become like a wineskin in the smoke,
> yet I have not forgotten thy statutes.
> *Psalm 119:83*

God does not interrupt his redemptive providences every time we lose sight of his ways in order to explain and prove what he is doing. He does not take time out to demonstrate the truth of his word every time we grow impatient. As a result we sometimes are plunged into obscurity—all dryness and doubts—and fear we can't make it. Nevertheless—because God *is*, we *can*.

PRAYER: Help me, God, to trust you even when I can't see clearly what you are doing. Help me to hope even when I cannot feel the conviction of your triumph. In the strong name of Jesus Christ. *Amen.*

286.
"Exceedingly Broad"

Read Psalm 119:89–96

> I have seen a limit to all perfection,
> but thy commandment is exceedingly broad.
> *Psalm 119:96*

Man's laws are relative and limiting; God's are "firmly fixed," "exceedingly broad." God's law is a firm center from which to begin; it is also a wide country in which to travel. It is solid and it is spacious.

PRAYER: I thank you, Father, for your word which has set me free from all confinement and released me from all restrictions. In your law I find perfect liberty to act and love in Jesus' name. *Amen.*

287.
"Makes Me Wiser"

Read Psalm 119:97–102

Thy commandment makes me wiser than my enemies,
  for it is ever with me.
  Psalm 119:98

As we develop understanding of the law of God, we gain skill in living in accordance with our own created nature and God's revealed will. The person who spurns this law can learn only by trial and error—a slow, painful and laborious process.

PRAYER: God, as people compete for my attention today, calling me here to learn a little of this, and there for a little of that, help me to keep my mind stayed on Christ. *Amen.*

288.
"Sweeter Than Honey"

Read Psalm 119:103–104

How sweet are thy words to my taste,
  sweeter than honey to my mouth!
  Psalm 119:103

The law of God is true. Each word is accurate and right. Each sentence is full of pleasure. The person who sits down to a banquet of such words knows all the nuances of joy. Such meals begin in delight and end in wisdom.

PRAYER: Praise God! Your generosity expands each pleasure; your grace puts dimensions that are past understanding into every delight; joy crowns every gladness. All your words are beatitudes. Thank you, in Jesus' name. *Amen.*

289.
"A Lamp to My Feet"

Read Psalm 119:105–112

Thy word is a lamp to my feet
and a light to my path.
Psalm 119:105

The Christian knows no more of the future than anyone else. But he does have clear illumination for each step taken in faith and hope—the daily steps of discipleship. For this reason the Christian strides into each day with confident joy.

PRAYER: "O grant us light, that we may know the wisdom Thou alone canst give; that truth may guide where'er we go, and virtue bless where'er we live. O grant us light, that we may see where error lurks in human lore, and turn our seeking minds to Thee, and love Thy holy Word the more." *Amen.*

(Lawrence Tuttiett, "O Grant Us Light")

290.
"I Hate Double-minded Men"

Read Psalm 119:113–120

I hate double-minded men,
but I love thy law.
Psalm 119:113

We must concentrate our devotion before we can expand it. We must harness our minds to the law of God before we can pull our weight of meaning and witness in the world. Jesus emphasized the same truth when he said, "If your eye is single, your whole body will be full of light" (Matt. 6:22, KJV, RSV).

PRAYER: I would look neither to the right nor the left, neither before nor behind, but keep my eyes on your word, O God. And then I would press on, single-minded, for "the prize of the upward call of God in Christ Jesus." *Amen.*

(Phil. 3:14)

291.
"Above Fine Gold"

Read Psalm 119:121–128

Therefore I love thy commandments
above gold, above fine gold.
Psalm 119:127

Christians know that the word of God, which costs them nothing
and which they can neither buy nor sell, is beyond value and at the
same time it shapes all other values. Our check stubs, the record of
how we spend our money, document the extent to which our values
are shaped (or not shaped!) by God's word.

PRAYER: You know, O Lord, how easily I am corrupted by the
world's values, how I judge people by their salaries and things by
their price tags. Purge me of all such baseness and teach me to value
everything in relation to your love revealed in Jesus Christ. *Amen.*

292.
"The Unfolding of Thy Words"

Read Psalm 119:129–134

The unfolding of thy words gives light;
it imparts understanding to the simple.
Psalm 119:130

When we first look at the word of God it is like a bud—a small
concentration of beauty. As we hold it before us in meditation it un-
folds, layer by layer, until the full flower is in blossom ready to be
viewed in all its intricately related parts.

PRAYER: O Father, there is so much that I am eager to learn from
your word. I have seen so little, but that little has whetted my appetite for more. As I hunger and thirst for your righteousness fill me
with your Holy Spirit. *Amen.*

293.
"Streams of Tears"

Read Psalm 119:135–136

My eyes shed streams of tears,
because men do not keep thy law.
Psalm 119:136

When the Christian becomes aware of acts of rebellion against God
and shrugs of indifference to God among his neighbors, he feels them
personally, for they are against the law he loves and in relation to the
Christ who loves all men.

PRAYER: Dear God, I pray for my friends who appear to be indifferent to your ways and heedless of your love. I know that your word
continues to them as a word of invitation, direction and love. I pray
for their repentance and faith, through Jesus Christ. *Amen.*

294.
"Thy Promise Is Well Tried"

Read Psalm 119:137–144

Thy promise is well tried,
and thy servant loves it.
Psalm 119:140

No one is asked to believe the word of God on the evidence of a
slick brochure or the sales pitch of a smooth-talking witness. There
are centuries of evidence to show its consistent truth and working
power. There are no words among men that are so well-tried and
thoroughly tested as the words of God.

PRAYER: I have spent far too much time, Lord, in wondering if
your promises work. I ought to be spending my time testing them out.
By your grace I will do that today. Reveal to me the word you would
have me test in this day's belief and behavior. *Amen.*

295.
"I Rise Before Dawn"

Read Psalm 119:145–152

> I rise before dawn and cry for help;
> I hope in thy words.
> Psalm 119:147

"The early morning belongs to the church of the risen Christ" (Dietrich Bonhoeffer, *Life Together*, p. 41). Christians, from the beginning, have encouraged one another to offer their first words, their first thoughts, the first moments of silence each day, to the Lord of creation.

PRAYER: "As the sun doth daily rise, brightening all the morning skies, so to Thee with one accord lift we up our hearts, O Lord! . . . Praise we, with the heavenly host, Father, Son, and Holy Ghost; Thee would we with one accord praise and magnify, O Lord!" *Amen.*
("As the Sun Doth Daily Rise," Latin hymn, trans. by O.B.C.)

296.
"The Sum of Thy Word"

Read Psalm 119:153–160

> The sum of thy word is truth;
> and every one of thy righteous ordinances endures for ever.
> Psalm 119:160

Everything in God's word adds up—and the total is *truth*. We are not faced with scattered items of information and counsel which we acquire bit by bit and use as we find opportunity. The law is a comprehensive whole in which we understand our life and salvation in the fullness of God.

PRAYER: I am so apt, O God, to get hold of one corner of your truth and forget the rest. Keep me aware of the sweep and splendor of your law, all its parts and its wholeness, even as it is shown complete in Jesus, in whose name I pray. *Amen.*

297.
"In Awe of Thy Words"

Read Psalm 119:161–168

Princes persecute me without cause,
but my heart stands in awe of thy words.
Psalm 119:161

There are some who think they can turn the words of God into the cozy and commonplace and use them as household items in a kind of kitchen religion. The true listener, aware of the God of creation who turned back the waters and exploded Gomorrah, stands in awe of their power and majesty.

PRAYER: "Lord, the words Thy lips are telling are the perfect verity; of Thine high eternal dwelling, holiness shall inmate be: Alleluia! Alleluia! Pure is all that lives with Thee." *Amen.*

(John Keble, "God, the Lord, a King Remaineth")

298.
"My Lips Will Pour Forth Praise"

Read Psalm 119:169–172

My lips will pour forth praise
that thou dost teach me thy statutes.
Psalm 119:171

This grand meditation on the law gathers to a climax in a crescendo of praise. The law which orders our lives in dimensions of mercy and puts us in daily touch with the delights of grace is celebrated in praise that sings.

PRAYER: "Father of mercies, in Thy Word what endless glory shines; forever be Thy name adored for these celestial lines. . . . Divine Instructor, gracious Lord, be Thou forever near; teach me to love Thy sacred Word, and view my Saviour there." *Amen.*

(Anne Steele, "Father of Mercies")

299.
"I Have Gone Astray"

Read Psalm 119:173–176

> I have gone astray like a lost sheep; seek thy servant,
> for I do not forget thy commandments.
>> *Psalm 119:176*

We do not merely admire God's word—we *need* it: it is that which saves us. It is this same word which "became flesh" in Jesus (John 1:14–18). It is not a word to revere in a church; it is a word by which we are rescued from daily sin.

PRAYER: Father, I love your word and cannot do without it. I have wandering feet and require much watching. Lead me and guide me in the name of Jesus "the great shepherd of the sheep." *Amen.*

(Heb. 13:20)

300.
"Woe Is Me, That I Sojourn in Meshech"

Read Psalm 120

> Woe is me, that I sojourn in Meshech,
> that I dwell among the tents of Kedar!
>> *Psalm 120:5*

A man submerged in a culture swarming with lies and malice feels as if he is drowning in it: he can trust nothing he hears, depend on no one he meets. The longing for peace and truth sets him on a pilgrim search for wholeness in God. Dissatisfaction with the world of sin is preparatory to traveling in the way of discipleship.

PRAYER: God, in a world where more lies are told than truth, and where enmity is more common than peace, I thank you for your constancy and your fidelity. Give me the strength to be a peacemaker when those around me are scornful of your peace. For Jesus' sake. *Amen.*

301.
"I Will Lift Up My Eyes"

Read Psalm 121

> I lift up my eyes to the hills.
> From whence does my help come?
> *Psalm 121:1*

A look to the hills for help ends in disappointment; for all their majesty and beauty, for all their quiet strength and firmness, they are, finally, just hills. Faith's vision stretches beyond the hills to the God who made the hills, the Lord of heaven and earth.

PRAYER: "What God's almighty power hath made, His gracious mercy keepeth; by morning glow or evening shade His watchful eye ne'er sleepeth; with the kingdom of His might, lo! all is just and all is right: to God all praise and glory." *Amen.*

(J. J. Schütz, "Sing Praise to God Who Reigns Above," trans. by Frances E. Cox)

302.
"I Was Glad"

Read Psalm 122:1–5

> I was glad when they said to me,
> "Let us go to the house of the LORD!"
> *Psalm 122:1*

The Jerusalem temple in ancient times and the local church in our times alike gather and order a worshiping, praising people. Any road which leads to a congregation of God's people is traveled with a glad heart.

PRAYER: I give you thanks, most gracious God, for the church in which I worship, the care with which it was built, the devotion with which it is maintained, the ministering uses to which it is put. For all this I thank you, in Jesus' name. *Amen.*

303.
"Pray for the Peace . . . !"

Pray for the peace of Jerusalem!
"May they prosper who love you! . . ."
Psalm 122:6

Peace—the ordered wholeness which God creates—is possible for cities as well as for individuals. What begins in the soul extends to the social order. Prayers for peace are at the heart of all effective social and civic concern.

PRAYER: Hear my prayers, O God, for the peace of this city in which I live. I pray for the officials who govern it, for the men and women who work in it, and for the children who play in it. Order all our lives in the peace of Jesus Christ. *Amen.*

304.
"Our Eyes Look to the Lord"

Read Psalm 123

Behold, as the eyes of servants
    look to the hand of their master,
as the eyes of a maid
    to the hand of her mistress,
so our eyes look to the LORD our God,
    till he have mercy upon us.
Psalm 123:2

Servants who through years of oppression have learned to fawn and cringe before mean masters discover another kind of Lord—the Lord who pours forth mercy. For the person who has been treated with contempt and scorn, the lordship of Jesus Christ is the happiest of discoveries.

PRAYER: Great God: sometimes I come to you in tense desperation, other times in relaxed gratitude, but never in fear. Your mercy is so gracious and your lordship so blessed that I can only be filled with praise. *Amen.*

305.
"The Lord Who Was on Our Side"

If it had not been the LORD who was on our side,
  when men rose up against us,
then they would have swallowed us up alive.
                              Psalm 124:2–3

The person who stands alone against the forces of evil doesn't stand a chance. But, in fact, no one does stand alone; the Lord stands with his people, a stance confirmed in Jesus who said, "I am with you always, to the close of the age" (Matt. 28:20).

PRAYER: I bless your great name, Almighty God. I look back over past years and remember the help I have known from your hand. Thank you for your strength shared with me, for your power exercised in me, for your being on my side in Jesus Christ. *Amen.*

306.
"The Lord Is Round About His People"

Read Psalm 125

As the mountains are round about Jerusalem,
  so the LORD is round about his people,
  from this time forth and for evermore.
                              Psalm 125:2

Jerusalem was set in a saucer of hills. It was the safest of cities because of the protective fortress hills around it. Just so is the man of God surrounded by his Lord who "cannot be moved" (v. 1). Better than a city gate, better than a military fortification, is the presence of the God of peace.

PRAYER: "Christ be with me, Christ within me, Christ behind me, Christ before me, Christ beside me, Christ to win me, Christ to comfort and restore me, Christ beneath me, Christ above me, Christ in quiet, Christ in danger, Christ in hearts of all that love me, Christ in mouth of friend and stranger." *Amen.*

(St. Patrick)

163

307.
"Our Mouth Was Filled with Laughter"

Read Psalm 126:1–3

When the LORD restored the fortunes of Zion,
we were like those who dream.
Then our mouth was filled with laughter,
and our tongue with shouts of joy.
Psalm 126:1–2

Every regathering in Jerusalem—the great homecomings which
were the feasts—recalled the mighty restorations that God had ef-
fected in Israel: out of Egyptian bondage, out of Babylonian exile.
The acts of restoration were impossible miracles. There was no way
they could have happened—"we were like those who dream." And
yet they did happen; the laughter, the shouts of joy, and the hymns
were present evidence.

PRAYER: I renew the memories of your work, O God, and know that
whatever ills or trouble I fall into, there is a way out in Jesus Christ.
I celebrate what you did in the past, and I anticipate what you will
do in the future. *Amen.*

308.
"Bringing His Sheaves"

Read Psalm 126:4–6

He that goes forth weeping,
bearing the seed for sowing,
shall come home with shouts of joy,
bringing his sheaves with him.
Psalm 126:6

The "watercourses of the Negeb" (v. 4) were a network of ditches
cut into the dry soil of Palestine's southland by wind and rain ero-
sion. For most of the year they were baked dry under the sun, but a
sudden rain would produce torrents of water and then a desert ablaze
with blossom. With such suddenness are long, dry periods of waiting
interrupted by God's invasion into our lives in Jesus Christ.

PRAYER: Let the rain of your Spirit fall on the dry soil of my heart,
O God. Bring to blossom the seeds which have been dormant in my
desert body. Restore, revive, replenish so that I may be a harvest·
field of "shouts of joy" for Jesus' sake. *Amen.*

309.
"The Bread of Anxious Toil"

Read Psalm 127:1–2

> It is in vain that you rise up early
> and go late to rest,
> eating the bread of anxious toil;
> for he gives to his beloved sleep.
> *Psalm 127:2*

Relentless, compulsive work habits, which our society tends to reward and admire, are seen by the psalmist as a sign of weak faith and assertive pride—as if God could not be trusted to accomplish his will, as if man could rearrange the universe by his own effort.

PRAYER: Teach me, O Lord, how to work steadily, faithfully and modestly. I know, Lord, that it is not a question of working or not working; it is a question of who is in charge. Is it going to be your work or mine? *Amen.*

310.
"His Quiver Full"

Read Psalm 127:3–5

> Like arrows in the hand of a warrior
> are the sons of one's youth.
> Happy is the man who has
> his quiver full of them!
> *Psalm 127:4–5*

The efforts of men who, in doubt of God's providence and mistrust of man's love, seek their own gain by godless struggles, are exchanged for the gifts of God, exemplified in the sons which are born, not through human toil or ingenuity, but through the miraculous processes of reproduction that God has created in us.

PRAYER: God, all that is most real and most personal in life—sons and daughters, friends and neighbors, parents and spouse—is provided through your creation, not by my struggle. What you have given so miraculously help me to enjoy gratefully. In Jesus' name. *Amen.*

311.
"You Shall Be Happy"

Read Psalm 128

You shall eat the fruit of the labor of your hands;
you shall be happy, and it shall be well with you.
Psalm 128:2

Everyone wants to be happy; not everyone is willing to participate in the conditions of happiness. God provides the environment for the happy life: his ways and his presence are the context in which we experience the happiness that lasts.

PRAYER: Father in heaven, I want your presence to become such a natural part of my life that all my acts are motions of obedience and all my words are accented with praise, so that I may experience the prosperity you have for me in Jesus Christ. *Amen.*

312.
"The Plowers Plowed Upon My Back"

Read Psalm 129

The plowers plowed upon my back;
they made long their furrows.
Psalm 129:3

If God's people participate in exceptional blessings (Psalm 128) they also suffer extraordinary afflictions. Neither cancels out the other; they exist side by side in the life of faith. Both joys and sufferings are redeemed by the Lord who lived and died for us in Jesus Christ.

PRAYER: I know that I am not the first one to feel pain and to suffer, O God, but while it is happening to me I feel as if I am. I look to you for comfort, strength and a final day when you will set all things right, through Jesus Christ. *Amen.*

313.
"Out of the Depths"

Out of the depths I cry to thee, O LORD!
Lord, hear my voice!
Psalm 130:1–2

There is no trouble so severe that it cuts a person off from God; there is no sin so powerful that it removes a person from the greater power of forgiveness. The witness of the troubled, suffering and afflicted who prayed and found their lives changed by a loving God is encyclopedic.

PRAYER: "Lord, from the depths to Thee I cried: my voice, Lord, do Thou hear: unto my supplication's voice give an attentive ear. . . . I wait for God, my soul doth wait, my hope is in His word. More than they that for the morning watch, my soul waits for the. Lord." *Amen.*

(*Scottish Psalter*, "Lord, from the Depths")

314.
"I Wait for the Lord"

Read Psalm 130:5–6

I wait for the LORD, my soul waits,
and in his word I hope.
Psalm 130:5

The long watches of the night through which soldiers guard cities and shepherds watch over flocks are compared with the wait of the soul before God. It is not the waiting of indolence but of alertness. Waiting is vigilance plus expectation; it is wide awake to God.

PRAYER: You, Lord, commanded disciples to watch and pray, and not long after you found them sleeping. I have similarly failed to stay awake to your commands and alert to your presence. Forgive my sluggishness and help me to make the most of the time. *Amen.*

315.
"He Will Redeem"

Read Psalm 130:7–8

O Israel, hope in the LORD!
For with the LORD there is steadfast love,
and with him is plenteous redemption.
And he will redeem Israel
from all his iniquities.
Psalm 130:7–8

Persevering prayer leads to forgiveness, unfailingly. No prayer is more sure of being answered than the prayer for forgiveness; no promise is more sure of fulfillment than the promise of redemption. Intensely felt need is the harbinger of a wholly accomplished salvation.

PRAYER: Father, into the depths of my need—my sin, my loneliness, my guilt, my failure, my inadequacy—let down the rope of your redemption and pull me to the heights where I may live completed and whole in Jesus Christ. *Amen.*

316.
"A Child Quieted"

Read Psalm 131

But I have calmed and quieted my soul,
like a child quieted at its mother's breast;
like a child that is quieted is my soul.
Psalm 131:2

An infant, noisy with hunger needs, is indifferent to talk and impatient with diversions but is quickly quieted when put to the mother's breast. Faith finds just such secure intimacy and satisfying nourishment in repose upon God.

PRAYER: How many times, dear God, have I gone to the pretentious words of men or to the promising diversions of the world to have my needs met? I am learning by your grace simply to come to you in quietness and faith, in Jesus' name. *Amen.*

317.
"Go to Thy Resting Place"

Read Psalm 132:1–10

Arise, O LORD, and go to thy resting place,
thou and the ark of thy might.

Psalm 132:8

King David centered the life of the Hebrew people in Jerusalem by bringing the ark of the covenant there. Every subsequent trip to the city followed ancient footsteps of pilgrimage, arousing memories which incorporated rich strains of praise into present obedience.

PRAYER: However lonely it seems, I know, O Lord, that this pilgrim way is well-trod and that I am not the first to encounter its difficulties. I look forward to the time when I complete my course and, with the great company of your people, offer final praise through Jesus Christ. *Amen.*

318.
"The Lord Swore to David a Sure Oath"

Read Psalm 132:11–18

The LORD swore to David a sure oath
from which he will not turn back:
"One of the sons of your body
I will set on your throne."

Psalm 132:11

Worship which begins by making resolves and offering petitions (vv. 1–10) concludes by receiving promises. We bring our moral best to the Lord, determined to "do something" for him, and then find that our zeal pales in insignificance before God's word to us. It is God who has something great to do for us, not we for him.

PRAYER: All your promises, God, reverberate through my soul— your blessing, your satisfactions, your salvation, your joy, your glory. I praise you for what you bring to me in Jesus Christ and worship in triumph. *Amen.*

319.
"When Brothers Dwell in Unity"

Read Psalm 133

Behold, how good and pleasant it is
when brothers dwell in unity!
Psalm 133:1

Glistening oil running down Aaron's beard and refreshing dew from the cool northern mountains are two pictures (the first of how it looks, the second of how it feels) of a community in which men and women find themselves forgiven by God and open in love to each other.

PRAYER: Father, break down every barrier that my sin builds between me and others: barriers of envy, of pride, of inadequacy, of scorn. Then let me see and feel the pleasures of sharing the inner delights of forgiveness and grace with the others whom you are gathering into your family. In Jesus' name. *Amen.*

320.
"Come, Bless the Lord"

Read Psalm 134

Come, bless the LORD,
all you servants of the LORD,
who stand by night in the house of the LORD!
Psalm 134:1

The people arrive at the place of worship and the cry goes out: "Come, bless the Lord!" Would some forget why they had come and spend their time socializing or trading? Would others suppose that the pilgrimage was its own reward and settle back, waiting for others to carry on the acts of worship? The song cues the blessing for which the journey was begun.

PRAYER: "Bless, O my soul! the living God; call home thy thoughts that rove abroad; let all the powers within me join in work and worship so divine. . . . Let the whole earth His power confess, let the whole earth adore His grace; the Gentile with the Jew shall join in work and worship so divine." *Amen.*

(Isaac Watts, "Bless, O My Soul! The Living God")

321.
"Sing to His Name, For He Is Gracious!"
Read Psalm 135:1–4

Praise the Lord, for the Lord is good;
sing to his name, for he is gracious!
Psalm 135:3

Firmly and deeply embedded in a biblical faith is the impulse to praise. Subterranean energies erupt through surface routines. "The Christian," wrote St. Augustine, "is an Alleluiah from head to foot!"

Prayer: "Father, Son, and Holy Ghost, help us to adore Thee, till, with all the angel host, low we fall before Thee; till, throughout our earthly days guided, loved, forgiven, we can blend our songs of praise with the song of heaven!" *Amen.*

(Cyril Argentine Alington, "Come, Ye People, Rise and Sing")

322.
"Whatever the Lord Pleases He Does"
Read Psalm 135:5–7

Whatever the Lord pleases he does,
in heaven and on earth,
in the seas and all deeps.
Psalm 135:6

High heaven, deep sea, and broad earth are hardly room enough for God to exhibit the dimensions of his good pleasure. Each recognition of the immensities of God gives additional scope to praise.

Prayer: I see you active, O God, in the small corners of my daily life and in the vast stretches of creation, in the minute affairs that occupy my mind and in the terrific reaches of eternity. Your will comprises small and great; your love embraces strong and weak. All praise to the Lord on high! *Amen.*

323.
"A Heritage to His People"

Read Psalm 135:8–14

The Lord gave their land as a heritage,
a heritage to his people Israel.
Psalm 135:12

The praising mind moves from the stuff of creation to the data of history. God is not only magnificent in what he has made, he is tremendous in what he does; he has made a glorious world and he acts out a stirring salvation.

PRAYER: Thank you, O God, for giving me a splendid world in which to live and for living in that world with me; for providing this place for living and then entering the process of living itself; for being both Creator and Savior to me, in Jesus Christ. *Amen.*

324.
"Like Them Be Those Who Make Them!"

Read Psalm 135:15–18

Like them [the idols] be those who make them!—
yea, every one who trusts in them!
Psalm 135:18

There are some kinds of sin from which one is more likely to be converted by laughter than by argument. Israel felt that way about idol-makers and idol-worshipers. Her favorite weapon against the pretentious absurdities of the idols was a good horselaugh.

PRAYER: God Almighty, I thank you for the ability to laugh at the ridiculous posturing of pride, for the perspective to see the clownish behavior of the arrogant. From insights gathered while laughing, build in me humility and loyalty as I serve you in Jesus' name. *Amen.*

325.
"Bless the Lord!"

Read Psalm 135:19–21

> O house of Israel, bless the LORD!
> O house of Aaron, bless the LORD!
> O house of Levi, bless the LORD!
> You that fear the LORD, bless the LORD!
> *Psalm 135:19–20*

While heritage, occupations and temperament divide us into different groups, worship gathers us into a whole community. In the act of worship we offer adoration and allegiance to God and find our differences joined in a community of praise.

PRAYER: Father, my needs and my experiences put me with people who feel the way I do; your commands place me with the people among whom you are working out a common purpose. Help me to become a participant with those who are praising what you have done, not congratulating one other on what they have done. In Jesus' name. *Amen.*

326.
"His Steadfast Love Endures Forever"

Read Psalm 136:1–9

> O give thanks to the LORD, for he is good,
> for his steadfast love endures for ever.
> *Psalm 136:1*

The leader of worship calls out a word of praise to God, each sentence an improvised elaboration of what God is and does; the people respond in unison with the reason ("for his steadfast love endures forever") linking each result to its cause. Every act of worship is just such a combination of diversity and continuity.

PRAYER: Thank you, O God, for your mercies which are "new every morning," and for your nature which is "the same yesterday and today and for ever." I never know what to expect from you; and yet I always know what to expect from you. You have so many ways of declaring redemptive love to me, but always it is redemptive love you bring, even through Jesus Christ. *Amen.*

(Lam. 3:23; Heb. 13:8)

327.
"Who Divided the Red Sea"

Read Psalm 136:10–22

[Give thanks] to him who divided the Red Sea in sunder,
for his steadfast love endures for ever.
Psalm 136:13

History is a museum through which the praising man can stroll, finding down every corridor evidence of what God has done in judgment and deliverance. Everything he observes is inserted in the story of praise and labeled as an exhibit of "steadfast love."

PRAYER: God, give me a mind as relentless as this psalmist's in discovering instances of your steadfast love, I want no gaps in my praise and no blanks in my thanksgiving. *Amen.*

328.
"O Give Thanks"

Read Psalm 136:23–26

O give thanks to the God of heaven,
for his steadfast love endures for ever.
Psalm 136:26

The phrase "his steadfast love endures forever" has been repeated twenty-six times in this psalm. Will the repetitions dull our minds into a pious stupor? Or will they condition the reflexes of our spirits to respond with quick praise to any stimulus?

PRAYER: O God, you do so many things in so many places—and I miss so much of it. I am lethargic in my responses, unbelieving in my reactions. I want to be more alive to the world of grace, more alert to the motions of mercy, more responsive to the descent of the Spirit. *Amen.*

329.
"By the Waters of Babylon"

Read Psalm 137:1–6

By the waters of Babylon, there we sat down and wept,
when we remembered Zion.
Psalm 137:1

The Hebrew exiles, despondent beside Babylonian canals, are taunted by passersby: "You people who are so famous for songs of praise, sing us one of your happy Zion tunes!" And they, homesick with longing, thought they couldn't do it. But they learned to when they realized that their Lord could be as precious to them in Babylon as he ever was in Jerusalem.

PRAYER: At the very moment, Lord, when I think all is lost, that there is nothing to be done, that defeat is total, show me the way of resurrection whereby you can bring new life, new song and new hope. In my Babylonian moods keep the vision of Jerusalem alive in my heart and teach me new songs of praise. *Amen.*

330.
"You Devastator!"

Read Psalm 137:7–9

O daughter of Babylon, you devastator!
Happy shall he be who requites you
with what you have done to us!
Psalm 137:8

This chilling imprecation, a seething torrent of hate and vengeance, seems like a blot on the pages of scripture. But "the ferocious parts of the Psalms serve as a reminder that there is in the world such a thing as wickedness and that it (if not its perpetrators) is hateful to God" (C. S. Lewis, *Reflections on the Psalms,* p. 33).

PRAYER: Father in heaven, as I seek ways to express your word of salvation to the sinner, keep me at the same time vigilant and hostile to sin so that even as I learn to love the persons you love, I may learn to hate the sins that you hate. *Amen.*

331.
"Strength of Soul"

Read Psalm 138:1–3

> On the day I called, thou didst answer me,
> my strength of soul thou didst increase.
> *Psalm 138:3*

The soul that praises God develops sinews of strength. Without praise our spirits become anemic and flabby. Praise stretches us to respond to God at full capacity and gives heartiness to faith.

PRAYER: Mighty God, in the same way that some develop their bodies in calisthenics and games, I will develop my soul in worship and praise. I don't want any part of my life to be weak resignation; I want all of it, by your grace, to be strong affirmation—a firm yes to your Yes to me in Jesus Christ. *Amen.*

332.
"All the Kings"

Read Psalm 138:4–6

> All the kings of the earth shall praise thee, O LORD,
> for they have heard the words of thy mouth.
> *Psalm 138:4*

Praise is not a private hobby, an avocation to be indulged in at leisure; it is a public affirmation, a powerful witness to God's ways and a celebration of his goodness.

PRAYER: "Mighty God, while angels bless Thee, may a mortal sing Thy name? Lord of men as well as angels, Thou art every creature's theme. Lord of every land and nation, ancient of eternal days, sounded through the wide creation be Thy just and endless praise." *Amen.*

(Robert Robinson, "Mighty God, While Angels Bless Thee")

333.
"The Midst of Trouble"

Read Psalm 138:7–8

Though I walk in the midst of trouble,
  thou dost preserve my life;
thou dost stretch out thy hand against the wrath of my enemies,
  and thy right hand delivers me.

Psalm 138:7

The themes of praise are vast and the subjects of praise are glorious, but its accents are always individual and personal: a prayer has been answered, a need has been fulfilled, a sin has been forgiven, a life has been made whole.

PRAYER: I thank you, dear God, for what you have done in my body and my spirit. I know that heaven and earth cannot exhaust your being nor even contain your wonders, but it is what you do in me that makes me want to praise what you do everywhere for everyone, through Jesus Christ. *Amen.*

334.
"Searched Me and Known Me!"

Read Psalm 139:1–6

O LORD, thou hast searched me and known me!
Thou knowest when I sit down and when I rise up;
  thou discernest my thoughts from afar.

Psalm 139:1–2

Any true life of the spirit must be narrated as a story of God's search for man, not man's search for God. God makes the first move; he understands our being and is conversant with our most personal inner life. His seeking removes all the panic from faith and all the anxiety from hope. All our works can be response and all our words praise.

PRAYER: "I sought the Lord, and afterward I knew He moved my soul to seek Him, seeking me; it was not I that found, O Savior true; no, I was found of Thee." *Amen.*

(Anonymous, "I Sought the Lord")

335.
"Whither Shall I Flee from Thy Presence?"

Read Psalm 139:7–12

Whither shall I go from thy Spirit?
Or whither shall I flee from thy presence?
Psalm 139:7

God cannot be avoided. We do not escape him by staying away from church or running away from home. We do not put distance between him and us by retreating to the mountains or adventuring across the seas. Always and everywhere he is the one with whom we have to do.

PRAYER: God, when I am lonely I want you to be close to me but feel you are far away; when I am guilty I want you to be far away but can't escape the sense of your presence. My feelings, I know, have little to do with the reality of your presence. Thank you for being with me to bless and not condemn, to comfort and not accuse, even in Jesus Christ. *Amen.*

336.
"Intricately Wrought"

Read Psalm 139:13–18

Thou knowest me right well;
my frame was not hidden from thee,
when I was being made in secret,
intricately wrought in the depths of the earth.
Psalm 139:14–15

The mysteries of conception and birth, the marvels of sinewed bone and muscle, provoke awe: God made this! I am evidence of God's skill! I am proof of God's creation! "Every man carries in his own body reasons enough for reverent gratitude" (Alexander Maclaren, *The Psalms,* 2:388).

PRAYER: Father, I have complained about my body when I ought to thank you for it. I have grumbled at its pains and been dissatisfied with its shape. Bring me to a state of shocked wonder at its intricacies, in awe of its marvels. Into a body not dissimilar to mine, and into flesh constituted like mine, you entered, O God, for my salvation. I praise you for it because of and through Jesus Christ. *Amen.*

337.
"Search Me, O God"

Read Psalm 139:19–24

Search me, O God, and know my heart!
Try me and know my thoughts!
Psalm 139:23

The all-knowing eye of God and his relentless pursuit are not inter-
ferences to be avoided but a companionship to be welcomed. God's
knowledge of me and his presence with me bring understanding and
freedom. In his light we see light (Ps. 36:9).

PRAYER: Lord, I see through a glass darkly; I am full of ob-
scurities and shadows. You are the light of the world. Show me what
I am in the light of your love so that I may find myself in your way
and in your salvation. *Amen.*

338.
"Preserve Me from Violent Men"

Read Psalm 140:1–5

Deliver me, O LORD, from evil men;
preserve me from violent men,
Psalm 140:1

Persecution, far from destroying faith, develops it. Hostile attempts against the faith are as futile as trying to get rid of a nail
by hitting it with a hammer—blows only embed it more firmly in
reality.

PRAYER: Powerful and merciful Savior, keep me from evil today.
When I am weak give me strength; when I am tempted grant me
courage; when I am disheartened provide me with hope. In the name
of Jesus who "himself has suffered and been tempted." *Amen.*

(Heb. 2:18)

339.
"My Strong Deliverer"

Read Psalm 140:6–8

O LORD, my Lord, my strong deliverer,
thou hast covered my head in the day of battle.
Psalm 140:7

Our needs do not exhaust divine help. There are no limitations to grace. Always there is strength for overcoming. "The prince of darkness grim, we tremble not for him; his rage we can endure, for lo! his doom is sure; one little word shall fell him" (Martin Luther, "A Mighty Fortress Is Our God").

PRAYER: "No more we doubt Thee, Glorious Prince of life! Life is nought without Thee; aid us in our strife; make us more than conquerors, through Thy deathless love; bring us safe through Jordan to Thy home above. Thine is the glory, risen, conquering Son; endless is the victory Thou o'er death hast won." *Amen.*
(Edmond Budry, "Thine Is the Glory," trans. by Richard Birch Hoyle)

340.
"The Cause of the Afflicted"

Read Psalm 140:9–13

I know that the LORD maintains the cause of the afflicted,
and executes justice for the needy.
Psalm 140:12

The ways in which man and God use power are set in contrast. Power *corrupts* man—when he has the means to assert his lusts and desires over others he very frequently does it. But power *expresses* God—he has the means to lift up the fallen and restore the ruined, and this he continuously does.

PRAYER: I welcome every manifestation of your power, Almighty God. Reestablish in my life the old orders of justice and peace, righteousness and love. Free me from the power of sin and release in me the power of your salvation. *Amen.*

341.
"Make Haste to Me!"

Read Psalm 141:1–2

> I call upon thee, O LORD; make haste to me!
> Give ear to my voice, when I call to thee!
>
> *Psalm 141:1*

Arrow prayers—petitions shot off to God on the spur of the moment—are spontaneous and urgent. The use of incense to symbolize prayer and the appointing of an evening hour for the sacrificial act of worship are legitimate enough, but prayer cannot be confined to such established forms and set times. Empty hands and unstudied words are always welcome before God.

PRAYER: Lord, take the half-formed sentences I address to you and the half-conscious movements I make towards you—my interjections and my gestures—and make prayers of petition and praise out of them, in the name of and for the sake of Jesus Christ. *Amen.*

342.
"Set a Guard Over My Mouth"

Read Psalm 141:3–4

> Set a guard over my mouth, O LORD,
> keep watch over the door of my lips!
>
> *Psalm 141:3*

Spontaneity in prayer develops intimacy with God. But gossip and rumor (saying whatever comes into our minds without considering the consequences) are also products of spontaneity. We are encouraged to cultivate open, uncensored speech with God; it does not follow that our speech with men should be without restraint. "From the same mouth come blessing and cursing. My brethren, this ought not to be so" (James 3: 10).

PRAYER: "Let the words of my mouth and the meditation of my heart be acceptable in thy sight, O Lord, my rock and my redeemer." *Amen.*

(Ps. 19:14)

343.
"The Word of the Lord Is True"

Read Psalm 141:5–7

When they are given over to those who shall condemn them,
then they shall learn that the word of the LORD is true.
Psalm 141:6

There are disciplines and difficulties that are associated with the "way of the righteous" (Ps. 1:6). And there are luxuries and delights which come only in alliance with the wicked. But faith plots its way, not on the basis of what feels good and not on the grounds of what looks good, but by compass readings from the "word of the Lord."

PRAYER: Father in heaven, you never promised that faith would be easy or popular, only that it would be whole and eternal. Keep me faithful to you and guided by your word, so that I will always prefer the bracing rebuke of kindness to the oily flattery of wickedness. *Amen.*

344.
"My Eyes Are Toward Thee, O Lord God"

Read Psalm 141:8–10

But my eyes are toward thee, O LORD God;
in thee I seek refuge; leave me not defenseless!
Psalm 141:8

There are moments in the Christian day when we wonder if a brief vacation from discipleship isn't in order. Voices lazily suggest that things are not as urgent as we had supposed, that perhaps the night is not very far spent. Then a time of testing clarifies commitment; we are forced to decisions that cement our loyalty to Christ who bids us "watch and pray that you may not enter into temptation" (Mark 14:38).

PRAYER: You, O God, are both end and means: you are where I am going and you are the way I get there. Defend me from siren distractions, from "the lust of the flesh and the lust of the eyes and the pride of life" which would lure me from the way and after other gods. *Amen.*

(1 John 2:16)

345.
"No Man Cares for Me"

Read Psalm 142:1–4

> I look to the right and watch,
>   but there is none who takes notice of me:
> no refuge remains to me,
>   no man cares for me.
>
> *Psalm 142:4*

Trouble does its best work when it drives us to God. The discovery that man cannot or will not help us is not a disaster if, at the same time, it shows us that God both can and will help. That we are abandoned by man is not the last straw so much as the first step to the realization that God is our help and salvation.

PRAYER: In the empty places in my life, devastated by broken promises and vacated by faithless companions, come, Holy Spirit, as Companion and Comforter. I will use my times of trouble to receive the help that only you can give. *Amen.*

346.
"The Righteous Will Surround Me"

Read Psalm 142:5–7

> Bring me out of prison,
>   that I may give thanks to thy name!
> The righteous will surround me;
>   for thou wilt deal bountifully with me.
>
> *Psalm 142:7*

The very prayer that announces trouble as abandonment—an exile of spirit resulting from careless unconcern by others—anticipates a centering in community: "The righteous will surround me." God's acceptance and embrace are very often expressed through welcoming words and supportive acts in the community of the people of faith.

PRAYER: Lord Jesus Christ, be at my side at the moments I feel isolated and alone. Use my sin-induced loneliness to prepare me for a faith-created community. Lead me to brothers and sisters in faith who share a common need and express a shared devotion. *Amen.*

347.
"I Muse on What Thy Hands Have Wrought"
Read Psalm 143:1–6

> I remember the days of old,
> I meditate on all that thou hast done;
> I muse on what thy hands have wrought.
> *Psalm 143:5*

Life accumulates irrelevancies as a ship acquires barnacles. Each item seems harmless in itself, but in the mass they sink us into sluggish immobility. Then some trouble invades our inertia and forces reflection; we see our lives in relation to God ("I muse on what thy hands have wrought") and realize our primary needs ("my soul thirsts for thee").

PRAYER: God, too much of my life is deadweight—habit, routine, and duty that have become separated from you. Wake me to my essential, eternal relationships. I will go over again what I know of *your* ways and reorder *my* ways by what I learn in Jesus Christ. *Amen.*

348.
"My Spirit Fails!"
Read Psalm 143:7–12

> Make haste to answer me, O LORD!
> My spirit fails!
> Hide not thy face from me,
> lest I be like those who go down to the Pit.
> *Psalm 143:7*

We do not, in prayer, develop a stiff upper lip—a pose of stoical self-sufficiency. Rather, we learn an honesty that is able to admit weakness and confess need in the presence of the God who is able to revive and strengthen us. The psalmist, in Calvin's words, "makes a chariot to himself of the extreme necessity of his case, in which he ascends upwards to God" (*Commentary on . . . Psalms,* 5: 254).

PRAYER: I need you, O God. I cannot sustain meaning and purpose by myself. I don't have within me the stuff to make life whole. I run out of resources. I run out of strength. In my emptiness I wait for your fullness. "Fill me with life anew." *Amen.*

(Edwin Hatch, "Breathe on Me, Breath of God")

349.
"Who Trains My Hands"

Read Psalm 144:1–4

> Blessed be the LORD, my rock,
> who trains my hands for war,
> and my fingers for battle.
> *Psalm 144:1*

There is strength, massive and awesome, in God. But he does not reserve the strength for himself; he shares it with his people. He is a stronghold in which we find refuge, but he also makes us strong in the fight of faith.

PRAYER: God my rock, train me in obedience and witness which will express your strong love and your victorious salvation, so that I am equipped to do battle in your name under the banner of your love. *Amen.*

350.
"Flash Forth the Lightning"

Read Psalm 144:5–8

> Flash forth the lightning and scatter them,
> send out thy arrows and rout them!
> *Psalm 144:6*

The life of faith is not calm repose on a warm ocean of tranquillity; it is pitched battle on a field noisy with conflict. But it is not our battle so much as it is God's; faith discovers the signs of his action and celebrates the power of his salvation.

PRAYER: Victorious God, when I see the conflict rage, I grow fearful; when I see the proud grow arrogant, I become timid. Put new heart in me by surrounding me with the signs of your triumph, in the strong name of Jesus. *Amen.*

351.
"Upon a Ten-Stringed Harp I Will Play"
Read Psalm 144:9–11

I will sing a new song to thee, O God;
upon a ten-stringed harp I will play to thee.
Psalm 144:9

Music is as much a part of battle as armor. Harps that fortify spirits have as much place as swords that maim bodies. Sounds as ancient and diverse as the skirling of Highlander bagpipes and the rallying rhythms of fife and drum are caught up and recast in the resurrection melodies that Christians sing in triumph over sin and death.

PRAYER: For weapons of faith to do battle in your name and for tunes of faith to sing the triumphs of your grace, I give you thanks, Almighty God, "who gives us the victory through our Lord Jesus Christ." *Amen.*

(1 Cor. 15:57)

352.
"Happy the People Whose God Is the Lord!"
Read Psalm 144:12–15

Happy the people to whom such blessings fall!
Happy the people whose God is the LORD!
Psalm 144:15

The conflicts, arduous and sustained, which Christians wage against temptation and for right have a victorious consummation: whole bodies, a bounteous land and a blessed people.

PRAYER: "A noble army, men and boys, the matron and the maid, around the Saviour's throne rejoice, in robes of light arrayed: they climbed the steep ascent of heaven through peril, toil, and pain: O God, to us may grace be given to follow in their train!" *Amen.*

(Reginald Heber, "The Son of God Goes Forth to War")

353.
"I Will Extol"

Read Psalm 145:1-3

> I will extol thee, my God and King,
> and bless thy name for ever and ever.
> *Psalm 145:1*

Praise raises a banner, blazoned with God's name and attributes, high into the air. Thrust against the sky, the celebrative flag catches the attention of the wandering and aimless and leads them in a parade of joy.

PRAYER: God, I want to fill the air with the notices of your goodness and attract drifting minds to a new allegiance to your lordship, even through Jesus Christ, my Lord and Savior. *Amen.*

354.
"One Generation ... To Another"

Read Psalm 145:4-7

> One generation shall laud thy works to another,
> and shall declare thy mighty acts.
> *Psalm 145:4*

Praise is antiphonal between the generations. Praises lifted in one century are echoed in another. Our voices pick up themes announced hundreds of years ago and add personal variations, producing "the voice of a great multitude, like the sound of many waters and like the sound of mighty thunderpeals, crying, 'Hallelujah!'" (Rev. 19:6).

PRAYER: Great and glorious God, what a choir I find around me. What rich themes of praise I can share. My voice with its thin sounds, unsure and imprecise, joins the great praises of the generations and I hear strong and harmonious sounds, resonant with grace. Hallelujah! *Amen.*

355.
"All Thy Works . . . All Thy Saints"

Read Psalm 145:8-13

All thy works shall give thanks to thee, O LORD,
and all thy saints shall bless thee!
Psalm 145:10

Praise is a collaboration between the material of creation ("all thy works") and the people of the covenant ("all thy saints"). Like a theater in which sets are constructed to enhance the dramatic speech of the players, the world is designed for the drama of blessing. As we discover the purposes and designs of God's work we find support and stimulus for praise.

PRAYER: God, help me to hear the praise which proceeds from things, from mountain shapes and rock textures, star tracks and sun warmth; and then let me add my "little human praise" to make a song pleasing to you. *Amen.*

(Robert Browning, "The Boy and the Angel")

356.
"Thou Satisfieth the Desire"

Read Psalm 145:14-21

Thou openest thy hand,
thou satisfiest the desire of every living thing.
Psalm 145:16

The diversities of God's goodness find root in the varieties of human need. Every discovered mercy in God finds application in human want. And every realization of human desire is an invitation to grace.

PRAYER: Father in heaven, I find my desires and needs an index to your will and promises. What I long for and require is what you bring to me in your steadfast love. Purify my desires and satisfy my being with the salvation in Jesus Christ. *Amen.*

357.
"Put Not Your Trust in Princes"

Read Psalm 146:1–4

> Put not your trust in princes,
> in a son of man, in whom there is no help.
> When his breath departs he returns to his earth;
> on that very day his plans perish.
> *Psalm 146:3–4*

Admiration is healthy: it is clear glass through which we see in others gifts and attributes to which envy is blind. But hero-worship introduces a distortion; it confuses the mere human with the near divine. Hero-worship is a first cousin to idolatry.

PRAYER: God of majesty, I would not confuse my admiration of persons whom I respect with adoration of you whom I trust. I will appreciate people but worship only you, in and through Jesus Christ. *Amen.*

358.
"Happy"

Read Psalm 146:5–10

> Happy is he whose help is the God of Jacob,
> whose hope is in the LORD his God.
> *Psalm 146:6*

Happy (sometimes translated "blessed") is used twenty-five times in the psalter. It is the first word in the first psalm; this is its last occurrence. It is one of the great and characteristic words for describing a person who centers life in God and experiences salvation by faith.

PRAYER: Lord, I thank you for the wide margins of happiness that border the story of faith. Your kind command "be of good cheer" is easily obeyed when I find your love in all my making and my growing. *Amen.*

(Matt. 9:2; 14:27; John 16:33; KJV)

359.
"Abundant in Power"

Read Psalm 147:1-6

> Great is our LORD, and abundant in power;
> his understanding is beyond measure.
> *Psalm 147:5*

The power of God can be seen in the way he treats the most insignificant persons, gathering outcasts and healing the wounded. It can also be seen in the way he runs the universe, numbering and naming the stars. Such power, whether observed in minutiae or immensity, is simply awesome.

PRAYER: "All hail the power of Jesus' name! Let angels prostrate fall; bring forth the royal diadem, and crown him Lord of all. . . . O that with yonder sacred throng we at His feet may fall! We'll join the everlasting song, and crown Him Lord of all!" *Amen.*

(Edward Perronet, "All Hail the Power of Jesus' Name")

360.
"His Pleasure"

Read Psalm 147:7-11

> His delight is not in the strength of the horse,
> nor his pleasure in the legs of a man.
> *Psalm 147:10*

God's deepest delight is not surveying a well-created world but entering into relationships of love with his people. A well-furnished and generously blessed creation is but "the outskirts of his ways" (Job 26: 14)—the center is the love in which we respond to our Lord in reverent praise.

PRAYER: Help me, O God, to use my observations of your providence as introductions to acts of faith. I want to use what I see of your work in creation as stepping stones to your work of redemption in me, sharing your good pleasure. *Amen.*

361.
"He Scatters Hoarfrost"

Read Psalm 147:12–20

> He gives snow like wool;
>   he scatters hoarfrost like ashes.
> *Psalm 147:16*

Everything observable in the world is a cipher for discovering grace. Even the weather. The suddenness with which a field is changed from harsh wasteland to a landscape softly contoured with snow, and the speed with which a warm wind can transform an icy fastness to cascading streams demonstrate the quick power of God: "his word runs swiftly" (v. 15).

PRAYER: What I am really interested in, Lord, is not the weather but your word. You speak the word that changes my life from indolence to discipleship in Jesus Christ, in whose name I praise you. *Amen.*

362.
"Praise Him, All You Shining Stars!"

Read Psalm 148:1–6

> Praise him, sun and moon,
>   praise him, all you shining stars!
> Praise him, you highest heavens,
>   and you waters above the heavens!
> *Psalm 148:3–4*

All parts of creation are mustered for the work of praise. The reasons for praise are so manifold and the possibilities of praise are so multiform, that every voice is put to work. No part of creation is exempt from the requirements and privileges of praise.

PRAYER: With everyone else singing so heartily, Lord, let not my voice be silent. Assign me my part in the music, so that my joy, my *life* a song, will harmonize with the soaring melody of creation, to your praise. *Amen.*

363.
"Praise for All His Saints"

Read Psalm 148:7–14

> He has raised up a horn for his people,
>   praise for all his saints,
>   for the people of Israel who are near to him.
> Praise the LORD!
>
> *Psalm 148:14*

Praising God is the most democratic of all activities. But instead of reducing all to a common denominator (as many democracies do), it raises everyone to new excellence. The potencies of praise develop and amplify as new voices join the chorus.

PRAYER: I don't want to miss a note, great God, in the chorus of praise, not overlook anything praiseworthy, not forget any benefit, not slight anyone or anything in my advertisements of your glory. *Amen.*

364.
"High Praises of God Be in Their Throats"

Read Psalm 149

> Let the faithful exult in glory;
>   let them sing for joy on their couches.
> Let the high praises of God be in their throats
>   and two-edged swords in their hands.
>
> *Psalm 149:5–6*

The "faithful" shatter every modern stereotype of the pious saint. There is not a shred of timidity in them, not a vestige of solemnity about them—they whirl in dance, brandish swords and raise exuberant songs of praise as they use every resource of voice and body to express delight in the God who delights in them.

PRAYER: O God, forbid that I should ever turn your glorious gifts into something dull and humdrum. I want to be among your faithful who convincingly demonstrate the freedom with which you set us free, and exhibit the joy that can only be sung with a new song, in the name and Spirit of Jesus Christ. *Amen.*

365.
"Let Everything That Breathes Praise the Lord!"

Read Psalm 150

Let everything that breathes praise the LORD!
Praise the LORD!

Psalm 150:6

The psalter concludes in a cannonade of praise: booming salvos of joy shake the air with "artful thunder" (Ralph Waldo Emerson, "Merlin"). Every means (eight instruments are listed) is put to use for the great end. Every creature is enlisted as a voice in the climactic chorus.

PRAYER: "Glory be to him whose power, working in us, can do infinitely more than we can ask or imagine; glory be to him from generation to generation in the Church and in Christ Jesus for ever and ever. Amen."

(Eph. 3:20–21, *Jerusalem Bible*)

*   *   *

Then I looked, and I heard around the throne and the living creatures and the elders the voice of many angels, numbering myriads of myriads and thousands of thousands, saying with a loud voice,
"Worthy is the Lamb who was slain,
to receive power
and wealth and wisdom
and might and honor
and glory and blessing!"
And I heard every creature in heaven and on earth and under the earth and in the sea, and all therein, saying,
"To him who sits upon the throne and to the Lamb
be blessing and honor
and glory and might
for ever and ever!"
And the four living creatures said,
"Amen!"
And the elders fell down and worshiped.

Revelation 5:11–14

Sources and Permissions

Cyril Argentine Alington, "Come, Ye People, Rise and Sing," stanza used
by permission of Lady Lavinia Mynors.
W. H. Auden, *Homage to Clio*, New York, Random House, 1960.
Dietrich Bonhoeffer, *Life Together*, New York, Harper & Bros., 1954.
George Bernanos, *Diary of a Country Priest*, translated by Pamela
Morris, Doubleday Image Books, 1954.
The Book of Common Worship, Philadelphia, The Board of Christian
Education of the Presbyterian Church in the USA, 1956.
Edmond Budry, "*Thine Is the Glory*," translated by Richard B. Hoyle,
copyright World Student Christian Federation, stanza used by per-
mission.
John Calvin, *Commentary on the Book of Psalms*, translated by James
Anderson, Grand Rapids, Wm. B. Eerdmans, 1949; *Institutes of the
Christian Religion*, Philadelphia, Westminster Press, 1960.
G. K. Chesterton (1874–1936), "O God of Earth and Altar," copyright
by Oxford University Press, two stanzas used by permission.
Richard Eberhardt, "Great Praises," *Selected Poems 1930–1965*, New
York, New Directions Publishing Corp., 1965.
Harry Emerson Fosdick, "God of Grace and God of Glory," two stanzas
used by permission of Elinor F. Downs.
Georgia Harkness, "Hope of the World," copyright 1954 by the Hymn
Society of America, stanza used by permission.
Gerard Manley Hopkins, "The Wreck of the Deutschland," *Poems of
Gerard Manley Hopkins*, Oxford University Press.
Friederich von Hugel, *Letters from Baron Friederich von Hugel to a
Niece*, edited by Gwendolen Greene, London, J. M. Dent & Sons, 1958.
The Jerusalem Bible, copyright © 1966 by Darton, Longman & Todd,
Ltd. and Doubleday and Company, Inc., quotations used by permis-
sion.

C. S. Lewis, *Reflections on the Psalms*, New York, Harcourt, Brace & Co., 1958.

Martin Luther, *Luther's Works*, edited by Jaroslav Pelikan, St. Louis, Concordia Publishing House.

Alexander Maclaren, *The Psalms*, 2 vols., New York, A. C. Armstrong & Son, 1908.

Thomas Merton, *Bread in the Wilderness*, New York, New Directions, 1964.

The Psalter, Philadelphia, United Presbyterian Church, 1912. (A somewhat revised edition is available from Wm. B. Eerdmans Publishing Co., Grand Rapids, MI.)

W. F. Sparrow Simpson, "Cross of Jesus," copyright by Novello Publications, Inc., stanza used by permission.

Dylan Thomas, "Fern Hill," *The Collected Poems of Dylan Thomas, 1957*, New York, New Directions Publishing Corp., 1957, quotation used by permission.

Artur Weiser, *The Psalms*, Philadelphia, Westminster Press, 1962.

(Poems and hymns not listed here are in the public domain.)